A MANUAL ON COMMON STOCK INVESTING

BY JOHN L. ROTONTI JR.

ISBN: 1492924466
ISBN 13: 9781492924463

DEDICATION

This book is dedicated to my wife, whose initials spell AMOR.
I love you today, more than yesterday, and every day more.

TABLE OF CONTENTS

INTRODUCTION

I wrote this manual because I have so much to say on the topic of investing, but thus far, I have found few people eager to listen. Perhaps this is because investing successfully requires incessant study, strict discipline, and a willingness to make money slowly. In a word, successful investing requires patience! If you are looking to become an overnight millionaire, I promise you that you will not like this book (and chances are, at some point, you will also lose lots of money). But if you are serious about accumulating wealth over a long period of time, this short manual can get you started on an endeavor that will not only enrich your retirement account, but will also enrich your mind. By researching companies for investment, you will learn more about business, cycles, and industry dynamics than you will in business school, guaranteed. This is not a knock on business school. It's just that a two-year business degree cannot possibly expose you to the number of businesses you need to read about in order to truly understand what to buy and what to avoid and how to earn satisfactory returns on your invested capital. But don't worry, the work will "pay" off and it's a whole lot of fun.

Investing is putting your money somewhere today so that you have more of it in the future, to retire comfortably, pay your children's tuition, leave to your heirs, travel the world, give to charity, or do whatever else you want with it. Two primary types of investments are stocks (partial ownership of publicly traded businesses) and bonds (loans you give to the government or corporations).[1] By investing in U.S. Treasury bonds, you can earn an annual return (or yield) that is referred to as the "risk-free" rate. It is referred to as risk-free because there is a general consensus that the U.S. government will not default on its debt, meaning that the holder of the bond will continue to receive the annual interest payments along with the return of principal when the bond matures.[2] Whereas U.S. government debt is considered risk-free, investing in stocks is not risk-free, because a stock investor could potentially lose all his investment if the company goes out of business. This book will focus on investing in businesses through the purchase of common stocks.

Since stocks entail risk, you should invest in stocks only if you expect to earn an annual return higher than the risk-free rate. Therefore, the risk-free rate is a crucial component to valuing stocks.[3] Of course, investing in stocks does not guarantee you a higher return; it depends on what you buy, what you pay for it, and what you do with the stock once you own it (do you continue to build a position and buy more? do you hold? or do you sell?), and that is what this book is all about.

This book highlights what I believe to be 17 principles of successful investing, each principle having its own chapter. From years of study and practice, I found that successful investors have similar

---

[1] Real estate is a third primary type of investment. You can invest in real estate directly by owning a home, apartment building, commercial building, etc. You can also get your real estate exposure through the stock market by investing in real estate investment trusts (REITs), hotel stocks, or holding companies and private equity firms that have real estate investments.

[2] For more information on bonds please see footnote 99 in Appendix 1.

[3] The annual return (or yield) that an investor hopes to receive is his required rate of return (or the opportunity cost of his capital). Simply put, investors have various opportunities available for them to invest in, and an investor's job is to compare the attractiveness of these various alternatives. The opportunity cost of your capital is how much more you could have earned had you invested in a different opportunity than the one you invested in. For example, if an investor chooses to invest in a security yielding 4% versus an alternative that he thinks can provide 8% to 10% annual returns, then he is forgoing the chance to double his returns.

investing philosophies. They have remarkably similar views on everything from value to volatility, from contrarianism to concentration, and from predicting the future to preservation of capital (don't worry, you'll learn what these things mean shortly). Do they do everything in the same way? Of course not. But overall, their understanding of what constitutes successful investing and what doesn't is the same. Successful investors believe in these principles with great conviction. They strictly adhere to their investing strategies in good times and bad, knowing that in the long run, taking a business owner's perspective and buying something only when it is priced attractively will yield good results.

A brief note on the structure of the book. I chose the title I did because I wanted to write an introductory-level, easy-to-read book on how to invest successfully in the stock market. All successful investing is "value" investing, that is, buying something for less than it is worth and then selling it when it reaches full value or becomes overvalued. Willingly paying more than something is worth just because you think the price will continue to go up for a little while longer is not "growth" investing, as it is sometimes called. Rather, it's gambling and it's dangerous.

This book is only as advanced as it needs to be to serve its purpose: to familiarize you with the principles of how to make money in the stock market and to motivate you to pursue a lifelong study of business and investing. I tried to write the book so that someone without a background in business can grasp the concepts. This book is an introduction to the stock market and investing and should be used as a manual to guide your future studies and to help you distinguish between what works in investing and what doesn't. This book introduces you to what I believe to be principles of successful investing, but to be a knowledgeable and successful investor, you will need to read more than just this book. This book is the start of your journey, not the end. Take a look at my bibliography and additional readings to get an idea of the books and reports that had the most influence on me. In addition to reading hundreds of books on investing and business, I read two newspapers each day and I read hundreds of company filings each year. If you have the time and desire to do the homework, and if you understand businesses and can tell a good investment from a risky one, then investing based on the principles in this book should be fun and rewarding. But if you do not have the skills to value a business and identify attractive investment opportunities, then a diversified portfolio of stocks is the safest way (and the only way I recommend) for you to participate in the stock market. By far the cheapest way to invest in a diverse portfolio of stocks is to buy an index fund. An index fund will guarantee you market results, which over time have been exceptional. If the only thing you knew about investing was that putting your money in an S&P 500 index fund and keeping it there was a good idea, you would have beaten the average hedge fund (or hedge fund index) in eight out of the last 10 years. Think about that for a moment: if you knew absolutely nothing about accounting, valuation, and individual stock picking, you would have crushed the results of highly educated and quite brilliant professional money managers by doing nothing more than investing in a simple index fund. Such a strategy would require zero research (once you choose the fund) and near-zero fees.[4] Year to date in mid-September 2013, the stock market as measured by the S&P 500 is up 18%. Meanwhile,

---

[4] Wasik, John. "Hedge Fund Hijinks to Continue After SEC Move," available at http://www.forbes.com/sites/johnwasik/2013/07/11/hedge-fund-hijinks-to-continue-after-sec-move/ (9/13/2013) and "Going Nowhere Fast," available at http://www.economist.com/news/finance-and-economics/21568741-hedge-funds-have-had-another-lousy-year-cap-disappointing-decade-going (9/13/2013).

the Hedge Fund Research global hedge fund index is up about 4% and the equity hedge fund index is up about 7% for the year.[5]

This book is only as long as it needs to be. My goal is not to inundate you with too much information right off the bat. That would only confuse and possibly bore you. Rather, I simply want to introduce you to some basic principles that you can easily digest and use as a foundation (or springboard) for a lifetime of investment success. I designed the book to be read in a sitting or two. I suggest you spend more time reading about businesses than you do reading about investing; there are maybe 20 great investing books, but to be a great investor you must understand business. To understand businesses, you must read about them. Additionally, many of these principles are so clearly rational that only so many words are needed to get the point across. More words will only detract from their simplicity. By the end of the book, I hope you will see that buying good businesses for less than they are worth just makes sense. I hope you will see that having a long-term mentality just makes sense. I hope you will see that owning fewer rather than more stocks just makes sense (but only if you know how to identify the few businesses worth owning). I hope you will see that if you have decades before retirement, favoring falling stock prices to rising stock prices just makes sense. And I hope you will understand the awesome power of compounding interest and the role that emotions wield in stock market success.

I start each chapter with a short quote from an investing superstar to grab your attention and to stress a point. This book is in no way endorsed or supported by the investors that I quote. Many of my quotes come from Warren Buffett's letters to shareholders available at www.berkshirehathaway.com. However, Buffett's letters on

---

[5] Data available at https://www.hedgefundresearch.com/hfrx_reg/index.php?fuse=login_bd (9/13/2013).

Berkshire's website prior to 1998 are in HTML version and do not provide page numbers. Therefore, my quotes from his letters prior to 1998 do not provide a page number in the citation, but that's OK because you should read the whole letter anyway.

I discuss 11 companies operating in different industries to give you an idea of what to look for when analyzing investment opportunities. I evaluate the companies in varying degrees of detail depending on which principle I am discussing at the time. But this analysis does not appear until the end of the book and in the appendixes because I first need to introduce you to the concepts and skills that are needed to perform a thorough business evaluation. This analysis is not a recommendation to buy or sell stock in any of the 11 companies. The company analysis that I provide should not be considered complete, because I often only address those aspects of the company that relate to the investing principle that I am discussing at the time. Also, a company's fundamentals or its stock price could be drastically different when you read this book than they were when I wrote the book. I have included these company discussions for educational purposes only. Before making any investment decisions, you should perform your own research and consult a financial advisor.

I have also included five appendixes in the book. Appendix 1 explains stock returns and multiples (ratios) used for valuation purposes. Appendix 2 provides a primer on how to calculate the various metrics discussed in this book. Appendix 3 examines the annual reports from two different companies to illustrate how reading a company's filings is helpful in understanding industries and businesses and how specific businesses compete within an industry. Appendix 4 discusses the importance of maintaining an investing watch list and gives an idea of the minimum amount of information an investor should know about a company on his watch list. Appendix 5 gives a very brief (and incomplete) introduction to the balance sheet and income statement. If you are new to investing, I suggest you read Appendix 1 before you read Chapter 1, because Chapter 1 deals with valuation. Appendixes 2 through 5 are probably best read after you have finished the book. Once you finish this book, I urge you to use my bibliography and recommended readings to continue your lifetime of study. Last, please pay particular attention to the footnotes at the bottom of the pages. I use footnotes to provide additional explanations and to cite my research sources. These are the exact same sources I use to find winning stock ideas. Enjoy!!!

CHAPTER 1: VALUATION AND WHEN TO BUY

Remember to read Appendix 1 before moving on.

In the average negotiated business transaction, unleveraged corporate earnings of $22.7 million after-tax (equivalent to about $45 million pre-tax) might command a price of $250-$300 million (or sometimes far more). For a business we understand well and strongly like, we will gladly pay that much [this is a p/e ratio of about 11x-13x]. (Warren Buffett letter to shareholders from 1984)

A key tenet of value investing is that the stock market is not always efficient. This is a fancy way of saying that stocks are sometimes mispriced. In other words, stock prices do not always reflect a company's intrinsic (or true) value. Sometimes the market price of a stock (the price the stock is currently trading at) more or less accurately represents a business's true value, but other times a stock price is either too high or too low (either overvaluing or undervaluing the stock) based on the fundamentals of the underlying business.[6] A related tenet of value investing is that over time the divergence (if one

---

[6] Stock may be mispriced for various reasons. Perhaps the market participants are missing something like an undervalued asset on the balance sheet or perhaps the market has misjudged the future earnings potential of the business. Another reason a stock may be undervalued is because the whole market is selling off because of concern and uncertainty regarding a largely unrelated headline event (such as bickering in Congress) and individual stocks are getting pulled down with the rest of the market. Of course, the market could be right and you could be wrong, which is why performing thorough research and investing only in what you understand (both of which will be addressed later in the book) are so important to investment success.

exists) between a company's stock price and its true value will narrow as the stock price moves either up or down to trade in line with its true value. That is, the market will eventually realize that it is wrong in its pricing of the stock and will buy or sell the stock until the price accurately reflects the true worth of the business. This convergence can take days, weeks, months, or years, depending on how long it takes the market participants to realize the discrepancy exists and to trade accordingly. Understanding how to value a business will allow an investor to identify when a stock is selling below its underlying value, purchase the stock (buying low), and hold it until the stock price moves up to or surpasses its true value, at which point a value investor will sell (sell high) and profit from the stock price appreciation. Now I will discuss how to value a business.

If I were to come up with an alternative title for this book, it would probably be *Ten Times Free Cash Flow* (10x FCF). The reason for this is simple: I feel comfortable that paying no more than 10 times free cash flow for a good business will ensure that, in most cases, I am not overpaying. As this book will show, minimizing permanent loss of capital is so integral to successful investing that I am obsessed with not overpaying for anything. At 10 times free cash flow, I feel that I am paying an attractive (and possibly even a bargain) price for those cash flows, limiting the downside and leaving the potential for significant upside.[7]

Limiting the downside is the key part of this insight. Smart investors acknowledge that deriving a business's exact value is nearly impossible and that our rough estimate of value could turn out to be wrong. Therefore, we need to leave ourselves a cushion by buying at a meaningful discount to our estimate of true value. This cushion is often referred to as a margin of safety. The larger the discount to

---

[7] I started to focus more on using price-to-free cash flow of 10x as a measure of attractive valuation after studying Bruce Berkowitz.

value (the cheaper we buy the stock), the larger the cushion we put in place to brace our fall if something goes wrong.[8]

Inverting the price/FCF multiple provides us with the stock's FCF yield (an estimate of expected annual return). A 10% FCF yield (equivalent to a P/FCF of 10x) provides an appealing long-term investment opportunity when compared to the risk-free rate on a 10-year U.S. Treasury bond, which, according to YCharts (http://ycharts.com), has averaged about 6.6% (nominal or before inflation) over the last 50 years and today hovers around 2.5%.[9] Using the S&P 500 as a proxy for the overall market, stocks have provided 9.6% average annual returns over the past 50 years.[10] Thinking in terms of yield allows investors to compare a stock's FCF yield not only to the risk-free rate, but also to the yields of other fixed income alternatives (like investment-grade corporate debt and junk bonds) and to yields from investing in real estate (a real estate's cap rate is calculated as annual net cash flow divided by the purchase price of the property). All else being equal, whether you are dealing

---

[8] Value investors are fond of saying you can't get hurt falling out of a first-story window, meaning that when you buy a stock cheap, the market is already pricing in bad news for the company, leaving the stock little room left to fall. I'll attempt to draw this analogy out a bit more. Let's equate a one-story house (so the window is on the ground floor) with paying 10x free cash flow, a two-story house with paying 20x FCF, a three-story house with paying 30x FCF, and a four-story house with paying 40x FCF. When you fall out of a first-floor window, you don't have a whole lot of distance to fall. You may get bruised up a bit, but in the long run you'll be OK in most cases. The same goes for stocks. In most cases, paying 10x FCF or less leaves little room for the stock to fall if something goes wrong internally at the company or the overall market heads south. Falling out of a second-story window will hurt more, but you will most likely recover. But if you fall out of a third- or fourth-floor window (the equivalent of paying 40x FCF), it could take you years to recover, if you recover at all. Stocks selling at unrealistically high multiples (way above industry and market average multiples) have much further to fall than stocks selling at below average multiples. Remember this window analogy should you ever be tempted to pay a P/E or P/FCF multiple of 30, 40, or 50x. Falling out of a fourth- or fifth-story window can be deadly, and if not, it's going to hurt like hell.

[9] Seth Klarman's Preface to the Sixth Edition of *Security Analysis*, pp. xxxiv–xxxv.

[10] Calculated using the S&P 500 Return Calculator at Don't Quit Your Day Job. Go to http://dqydj.net/sp-500-return-calculator/ (8/27/2013) to find the return calculators for the S&P 500, U.S. Treasury bonds, and gold.

with stocks, bonds, or real estate, higher yields indicate cheaper purchase prices.

Price-to-free cash flow is one of various multiples used for valuation purposes (see Appendix 1). It measures the price you pay for a company's cash flows relative to the company's own history and relative to other companies in the market. There are ways to value a business other than using relative multiples. Seth Klarman discusses the different valuation methods better than I ever could in his epic book, *Margin of Safety*, and on pages xxxiv-xxxv of his preface to the Sixth Edition of *Security Analysis*, the seminal text on fundamental analysis and value investing co-authored by Benjamin Graham and David Dodd. To deeply understand valuation, I strongly encourage you to read Graham and Dodd and Klarman. I believe Klarman's chapter on "The Art of Business Valuation" and his detailed explanation of how he valued Esco Electronics Corporation in *Margin of Safety* should be required reading for anyone serious about value investing. But I will provide a very brief overview of the other ways to value a business here.

The first is to estimate a company's liquidation value, or what would be left over if the company sold off all assets and used the proceeds to pay off all debts. Book value is sometimes a good proxy for liquidation value and sometimes isn't. Deriving an accurate estimate of liquidation value can sometimes require getting appraisals for things like inventory, land, and real estate, and these appraisals cost money. As an alternative to paying for an appraisal, investors can often research recent appraisals of similar assets. For example, in September of 2013 the *Wall Street Journal* reported that J.C. Penney recently had its real estate professionally appraised at $55 per square foot.[11] Some investors may choose to use this $55 per

---

[11] Lahart, Justin. "Ringing Up the Sum of All Sears," available at http://online.wsj.com/article/SB10001424127887323864604579069424056364230.html (9/16/2013).

square foot as an estimated value of Sears's real estate portfolio. But the same *Wall Street Journal* article mentions another recent report that values Sears's real estate at $98 per square foot. Since I have absolutely no idea which appraisal is more accurate and since Sears's vast real estate holdings are a significant contributor to its overall value, Sears falls outside of my comfort zone (or what Warren Buffett refers to as a circle of competence). Quite simply, I do not know how to value Sears, so I won't invest in Sears. But for those of you who work in real estate as a developer, contractor, leasing agent, or commercial appraiser, confidently valuing Sears may be a lot easier for you than it is for me.

Liquidation value can be thought of as an adjusted book value (net asset value) because you are adjusting the assets on a company's balance sheet to more accurately reflect current economic realities. For example, land is often on a company's books at historical cost, or the price at which it was originally purchased. But if the land was purchased 50 or 100 years ago, it may be worth far more today and therefore may not be accurately valued on the company's balance sheet. I highly encourage you to read Bruce Greenwald and Joe Calandro, who, in my opinion, are the two masters on adjusted book value. Professor Jim Kelly, the director of the Gabelli Center for Global Investment Analysis and the director of the value investing program at the Gabelli School of Business at Fordham University, uses both Greenwald's *Value Investing* and Calandro's *Applied Value Investing* in his classes.

Another method of valuation is to apply takeout multiples from similar acquisitions to the company you are valuing to determine its private market value. Private market value is an estimate of what you think the company would sell for if it is acquired based on recent acquisition pricing in the same industry. Mario Gabelli has produced one of the most impressive long-term investing records using his proprietary method of valuation termed "private market value with a catalyst." A catalyst is an event that will bring attention to the underlying value of the company. Possible catalysts include mergers and acquisitions, favorable regulatory changes, a change in management (a new CEO), a change in capital allocation (the announcement of a large share-buyback program or substantial increase in the dividend), or special situations such as a spin-off (when a subsidiary becomes a separately traded entity) or a recapitalization (taking on a lot of debt to buy back a lot of stock).

A final way to value a business is to use the discounted cash flow (DCF) method. Theoretically, the value of any asset is the present value of its future cash flows (all the future cash flows for the life of the business discounted back to the present). The discount rate is the investor's required rate of return. I personally won't invest unless I expect 8% to 10% annual returns, because 10% is the long-run annualized return of the stock market (I want to do at least as well as the stock market). For a company that has a higher risk profile, I require higher returns to compensate for the additional risk, so I may use a 15% or 18% discount rate. In theory, a discounted cash flow model is a beautiful thing, but in reality discounting cash flows can be difficult because you need to make assumptions on the company's growth and margins far into the future, and those assumptions often prove wrong. But, at the very least, you should understand the theory of the DCF method and the time value of money.[12] For a step-by-step guide on how to do a DCF model, please

---

[12] Would you rather a dollar today or a dollar at some point in the future? The time value of money is based on the concept that a dollar today is worth more than a dollar in the future because you can invest the dollar today and earn interest on it. A dollar invested today is worth $1 plus interest a year from now. If interest rates are 5%, a dollar invested today will be worth $1.05 a year from now (1 x 1.05^1 = 1.05). That is the future value calculation. But a dollar received a year from now is worth less than a dollar today because you miss the opportunity to invest it today. Therefore, a dollar received one year from now must be discounted back to the present at the opportunity cost of your capital (which in this case is the 5% you could

consult any of Aswath Damodaran's many books on valuation and/ or *Valuation* by McKinsey & Company. Or read Robert Hagstrom's *The Warren Buffett Way.* By reading Hagstrom, you can kill two birds with one stone: he provides a very clear guide on valuing a business by discounting owner's earnings and I consider him to be the best author on Warren Buffett's investing strategy. I love his books, and when you check out my recommended reading list, you will see that I have three Hagstrom books on there.

Of all the methods discussed, I feel most comfortable buying businesses at very low multiples of free cash flow or book value. But, nothing is wrong with using multiple methods to value a business. If nothing else, diving in and working through a DCF and liquidation model and researching the takeout multiples of similar acquisitions will help you better understand the business and the industry it operates in.[13]

---

have earned had you invested the dollar today). Think about it like this: how much would you need in hand today so that if you invested it today (and earned interest on your investment) it would be worth exactly $1 a year from now? At a 5% interest rate, a dollar received a year in the future is worth only about $0.95 today (1 / 1.05^1 = 0.9524). This is the present value formula. Understanding this present and future value concept and how discounting works is an important building block of investment success. To summarize, the future value formula calculates how much money you will have in the future based on today's investment. The present value formula tells you how much money you need now in order to have a specified amount in the future. Also, the dividend discount model is similar to a DCF model, except it discounts dividends as opposed to free cash flows.

[13] The residual income model is another method of valuation that I have some experience with. I was first introduced to this method by Professor Deen Kemsley in my MBA program. Professor Kemsley was an incredible teacher who taught his students analysis tools that weren't taught in my other business school classes such as credit analysis, the DuPont method of understanding returns on equity, ways to measure earnings quality and how to spot possible accounting shenanigans, and the residual income model. The residual income model says that the value of equity is equal to the current book value plus the present value of all future residual incomes. Whereas with the DCF method you are discounting free cash flows, with the residual income method you are discounting future streams of residual income. Residual income is calculated as net income minus the cost of equity times shareholders' equity. Cost of equity is simply a shareholder's required rate of return. A positive residual income indicates a company is earning more than shareholders require based on their opportunity cost of capital (or their required rate of return). The residual income method is based on the premise that over time

Summary: One highly effective way to value stocks is to compare their free cash flow yields to the risk-free rate. If a stock's FCF yield is significantly higher (let's say 2x higher) than the yield on the 10-year U.S. Treasury bond, you may have found yourself a relative bargain.

---

positive residual income at most companies will fade to zero. The residual income method is helpful because it forces investors to consider how long a company will be able to maintain positive residual income in the face of increasing competition. But a drawback of this method is that it is also based on future assumptions (just like the DCF method). Another drawback is the large emphasis it places on accounting book value because it says a company with positive residual income is worth its book value plus a premium. Therefore an analyst must start by closely scrutinizing a company's reported book value and making any necessary adjustments to reflect current economic realities.

CHAPTER 2: WHAT TO BUY

The Fortune *[magazine] study I mentioned earlier supports our view. Only 25 of the 1,000 companies met two tests of economic excellence – an average return on equity of over 20% in the ten years, 1977 through 1986, and no year worse than 15%. These business superstars were also stock market superstars: During the decade, 24 of the 25 outperformed the S&P 500. (Warren Buffett letter to shareholders from 1987)*

I aim to buy quality companies. Quality's most vocal supporter is Warren Buffett, who prefers to buy great businesses at an attractive price and is often willing to buy a great business at a fair price. In his 2012 letter to shareholders, Buffett educates us on the importance of buying quality. He writes, "More than 50 years ago, Charlie told me that it was far better to buy a wonderful business at a fair price than to buy a fair business at a wonderful price. Despite the compelling logic of his position, I have sometimes reverted to my old habit of bargain-hunting, with results ranging from tolerable to terrible."[14] Paying a fair price (leaving you zero margin of safety) for an average or poor enterprise is not a good idea. Those are the types of businesses you need to buy real cheap (with a large margin of safety) because lots can go wrong. But paying a fair price for a great business is often a smart investment because great businesses have the ability to increase their intrinsic value over time. Businesses can increase their intrinsic (true) value by growing

---

[14] Warren Buffett letter to shareholders from 2012, p. 13.

earnings and free cash flows, increasing their returns on invested capital, and strengthening their competitive advantages and lead over the competition. These are all concepts you will learn about shortly.

The two most important measures of business quality are (1) the company's ability to generate strong free cash flow, and (2) the company's ability to generate and sustain high returns on equity (ROE) and returns on invested capital (ROIC). Return on equity is the return the company generates on equity holder investments, and return on capital is the return a company earns on both equity and debt holder investments (both equity and debt capital).

Free cash flow (FCF) is the amount of cash that a company generates after spending on capital expenditures (property, plant, and equipment) to maintain (maintenance and repair of existing machinery and facilities) and grow (building or acquiring new machinery and facilities) its assets. A rough measure of FCF can be calculated by subtracting capital expenditures from operating cash flow.[15] FCF is the actual amount of cash available to investors and can be used to reinvest back into the business, pay dividends, buy back stock, pay down debt, or make acquisitions. Any leftover free cash can be used to increase the cash on the balance sheet.[16]

---

[15] You can get additional definitions and calculations at http://www.investopedia.com/terms/f/freecashflow.asp (8/27/2013).

[16] Just like you or me, companies have alternative uses for their cash. One of the things they can do with their cash is buy back (repurchase) their own stock. Theoretically, a company should buy back its own stock for the same reason an investor would want to buy stock in that company: because it represents a good investment (it's a good use of cash). In other words, it's a way for the company to invest in itself. When a company buys back stock, it reduces the number of shares outstanding. Reducing the number of shares outstanding increases the earnings per share. So, at the right price, share repurchases are a great way to reward shareholders by building per share value. But companies often buy back stock for the wrong reasons, either to temporarily prop up the stock price or to simply avoid increasing the number of shares outstanding when they issue new shares via employee stock options. These additional shares dilute the percentage ownership of existing shareholders. Companies that buy back stock for these suspect reasons often do so regardless of where the stock is trading,

One way to determine if a company is a free cash flow-generating machine is to calculate the percentage of revenue the company is turning into free cash flow, a metric referred to as the free cash flow margin. Free cash flow margin is simply FCF divided by revenues. A FCF margin of 20% is very healthy, and a margin above 10% should raise your attention.

The other measure of quality is a business's ability to consistently generate high returns. Here's how to think about a company's return on capital: Profits should not be examined in a vacuum. A company's absolute dollar amount of profits should be compared to the amount of capital (investment) needed to generate those profits. In general, the best businesses are those that are not capital intensive, meaning they don't require a lot of money to constantly repair and replace aging assets (they generate cash rather than burning through it). The goal should be to maximize profits with the least amount of reinvested capital. As always, Warren Buffett provides clarity. In his 1980 letter to shareholders he says, "Increased earnings produced by increased investment don't count."

Businesses that consistently generate above-average returns on capital have a competitive advantage (sometimes referred to as a moat by Warren Buffett) that protects their profits from the competition. This advantage can take different forms. For example, a company may have a patent protecting its product (or technology) from the competition for up to two decades (think pharmaceutical companies charging high prices for patented drugs) or may have a

---

meaning that they end up paying more than the stock is worth. Paying more than something is worth is a bad move by any entity (whether it is an individual shareholder buying stock or a company repurchasing its own shares) and it destroys shareholder value. One way to see if a business is serious about share buybacks (or if it is just trying to offset dilution) is to see if the share count is going down over time. Examples of companies that are serious about buying back stock are DirecTV, Loews, Exxon Mobil, IBM, and Microsoft. Look at their share count over the last decade to see what I mean.

strong brand and intensely loyal following (think Coca-Cola, Heinz, Starbucks, and Rolex). These businesses, which can increase prices without losing customers, are better able to weather a storm of inflation and are somewhat insulated from the price wars that other industry participants may have to partake in. In other words, they have pricing power. Another type of competitive advantage is to be the low-cost producer, meaning that one company can produce (or source) the product for less money than the competition (think Wal-Mart and Costco). These companies can and do compete on price (offering lower prices) while still maintaining decent profit margins. Wal-Mart and Costco use their size (scale) to demand the lowest possible prices from their vendors, which allows them to offer very low prices to consumers. Real, long-lasting competitive advantages are rare, and they can strengthen, weaken, or even disappear over time.[17]

Warren Buffett's preferred measure of performance is return on tangible equity. Return on equity is calculated as net income divided by total shareholders' equity. Return on tangible equity is simply net income divided by tangible book value, where tangible book value is calculated as total assets less total liabilities (which is book value) less goodwill and intangibles. In his 2012 letter to shareholders, Warren Buffett defines "terrific" returns on tangible book value (return on tangible equity) as 25% or higher. He categorizes "good" returns as ranging from 12% to 20% and "poor" returns as anything less than 12%.[18]

Recognizing that a company has above-average returns on equity (ROE) is important. But to understand why they are generat-

---

[17] Warren Buffett letter to shareholders from 2007, p. 6. For additional information on competitive advantages, read Bruce Greenwald's *Value Investing: From Graham to Buffett and Beyond*, pp. 75-85.

[18] Warren Buffett letter to shareholders from 2012, p. 13.

ing higher returns than the industry, one needs to understand the drivers of ROE. ROE is driven by debt levels, profit margins, and asset turnover. Higher asset turnover (for example, selling inventory and restocking shelves multiple times per year) and higher profit margins lead to higher ROE. A company can also juice its returns by taking on debt. To better understand the drivers of ROE, I encourage you to research the DuPont method of analysis.

There are different ways to calculate return on invested capital (ROIC). In *The Little Book That Beats the Market*, Joel Greenblatt recommends using operating income (EBIT) divided by tangible capital employed, where tangible capital is calculated as net working capital plus net fixed assets.[19] Another common method is to divide after-tax operating income by long-term debt plus shareholders' equity. Once again, an ROIC of 20% or higher is generally considered strong.[20]

I get excited when I find what I call 20-20-10 businesses: those businesses with at least a 20% FCF margin and 20% ROE and priced with a 10% FCF yield. There are other fundamentals that need to be considered when buying a business, but 20-20-10 stocks are a great place to start.

Another great place to start is to find a business that you understand and admire and that has a simple investment thesis, advice that Warren Buffett, Charlie Munger, and Peter Lynch have preached for decades. But for one of my favorite quotes on this topic I will turn to an investor who is less familiar to many of us. On August 9, 1981, Dean Williams gave the keynote speech to the Financial Analysis Federation. In the speech, titled "Trying Too Hard," Dean Williams said, "The reasons for dwelling on the virtue

---

[19] Joel Greenblatt, *The Little Book That Beats the Market*, pp. 138-139.

[20] Don't worry, I will walk you through how to do all these calculations in Appendix 2.

of simple investment approaches is that complicated ones, which can't be explained simply, may be disguising a more basic defect. They may not make any sense. Mastery often expresses itself in simplicity."[21] If you take nothing else from me, remember this: Investments do not have to be complicated to be profitable. Quite the contrary, it is often the simplest ideas that produce the greatest long-term gain.

I suggest focusing your efforts on identifying quality businesses that you can purchase at attractive prices, but some deep-value investors focus on a security's cheapness. They don't want to pay a fair price for anything, since paying a fair price leaves the potential for more downside (if something goes wrong internally at the company or if there is a general market downturn) and less impactful upside. Value investing is, after all, buying something for less than it is worth. In general, deep-value investors place less emphasis on quality and focus more on buying cheap.[22] I assume that they would happily buy quality companies if they could purchase them at large-enough discounts to underlying value. Quality companies, however, rarely sell at the discounts that they require.

---

[21] Williams, Dean. "Trying Too Hard" (1981), p. 14, available at http://turnkeyanalyst.com/wp-content/uploads/2013/02/Williams-Trying_too_Hard.pdf (6/29/2013).

[22] Deep value investing is sometimes referred to as cigar butt investing or Dumpster diving. The idea of the cigar butt metaphor is that you can pick up a cigar butt on the street (buy a stock) for free, since you don't have to pay anything for it, and you may get one last puff out of it (you may get one last jump in the stock price) before it fades out. Dumpster diving is a similar concept. That is, you can jump into a Dumpster and you might find something semi-worthwhile like a discarded pair of sneakers or even a piece of half-eaten pie. Here's my take on this: I don't want to puff on someone else's used cigar and I sure as hell don't want to dive into a dirty Dumpster on the off chance I might find something of value. I view diving headfirst into a Dumpster in life the same way I view Dumpster diving for stocks: it's just too damn risky. The probability that I dive into a Dumpster and find a discarded winning lottery ticket is just not worth the risk or the effort in my opinion. The risk-reward just doesn't make sense for me. But the risk-reward may make sense for others, and some investors that play in this space have made a fortune.

In *The Most Important Thing*, Howard Marks explains, "A fundamentally weak asset – a less-than-stellar company's stock, a speculative-grade bond or a building in the wrong part of town – can make for a very successful investment if bought at a low-enough price."[23] I agree completely, but I'm just not good enough at determining which struggling companies won't just continue to struggle, and I'm not nearly as skilled as Marks at valuation and knowing when to sell. Howard Marks is an investing genius. I am not.[24] Therefore, I try to invest in the best of both worlds, buying great companies at what I consider to be great prices. Since I manage only my own money, I am willing (and able) to hold a relatively large amount of cash on the sidelines for months or even years, waiting for just the right opportunity. My personal investing goal is to build up meaningful ownership positions at attractive prices in some of the best companies in the world over a long period of time. But, make no mistake about it: price is the key ingredient of investment returns. Paying far too much for a great company can be detrimental to performance. Perhaps this is just wishful thinking, but I believe that quality and value (cheapness) are not mutually exclusive. Investors can find quality companies selling at cheap prices, but this strategy requires unusual patience and a willingness to invest big when opportunities present themselves (after all, I don't want my cash sitting on the sidelines forever).

Of course, others could argue that with the Internet and tech companies disrupting so many traditional business models, it is getting harder and harder to determine which companies are truly

---

[23] Howard Marks, *The Most Important Thing*, p. 37.

[24] Although I have read all of Howard Mark's memos at www.oaktreecapital.com and both of his books, I did not consult Marks on his views of quality and price. I am simply using this one quote to show that buying cheap assets, although they may not be considered high quality, can be a very profitable strategy and perhaps even the most profitable. It's just not something I'm particularly good at.

great, or at least which ones have truly great staying power. They are right; it is getting harder. Still, for me, evaluating which companies have durable competitive advantages is easier than determining which companies won't simply sink further into trouble. Turning a company around is difficult, but companies that have excelled in the past often (but not always) have the experience, finances, and culture to excel going forward.

Some investors place a little more emphasis on the fundamentals of the underlying business, and others place more emphasis on the price at which they can purchase a business. Some place a little more emphasis on the size of the "moat," and others place more emphasis on the size of the "margin of safety" (or discount to value). Some try to blend the two. This book highlights principles of successful investing, but that does not mean all successful investors will end up purchasing the same assets. Investing is a subjective process. Whereas strict value investors err on the side of caution by buying cheap, I err on the side of caution by buying fundamentally strong businesses that I understand, at valuations I consider cheap, but that may not always be considered cheap enough by more traditional value investing standards.

Here is another way to think about what to buy. Aim to buy above-average companies selling at below-average prices. Historically, the S&P 500 index has traded at a price-to-earnings ratio of about 15x-16x and a price-to-free cash flow of about 30x.[25] The index has historically traded at a price-to-book of about 3x.[26] Since the S&P 500 is a proxy for the stock market,

---

[25] According to S&P Capital IQ, from April 1991 to April 2013 the S&P average price/levered free cash flow was 34x and from January 2000 through August 2013 the average price/levered free cash flow was 29x.

[26] From December 31, 1999, through September 10, 2013, the average price-to-book of the S&P 500 was 2.8x according to http://www.multpl.com/s-p-500-price-to-book/table/by-year (9/10/2013).

we can assume that the average company in the U.S. trades at about 15x earnings, 30x free cash flow, and 3x book value. But, a company that has a history of consistently producing a lot of free cash flow and consistently generating high returns on equity (and returns on invested capital) is an above-average company. Above-average companies deserve to trade at above-average multiples. So, a fair price for an excellent business very well may be 18, 19, or even 20 times earnings (and maybe higher) or 3.5 or 4 times book value (and maybe higher). And very occasionally, the market will provide us with the opportunity to purchase a well-above-average company for a well-below-average multiple. When given this opportunity, buy the stock. Let me see if I can give you an example. On March 9, 2009, Warren Buffett was on CNBC's *Squawk Box*, where he told the world that American Express's stock price was undervalued.[27] At the time, American Express's stock price was about $10, its price-to-earnings ratio was about 5x (versus its current 5-year average p/e of about 16x), and its price-to-book ratio was about 1x (versus its 5-year average p/b of about 3x).[28] American Express has averaged 26% returns on equity over the past 10 years (12/2003 – 12/2012), but in 2009 it was selling at low single-digit multiples of earnings and book value.[29] It made absolutely no sense, and situations like that (which come around ever so rarely) are an investor's dream. Today, American Express's stock price is about $75, for a 650% return, not including dividends.[30] When Buffett speaks, we all should listen![31]

---

[27] http://www.cnbc.com/id/29595993 (10/11/2013).

[28] Source: YCharts.

[29] In the 6 years (12/2003 – 12/2008) prior to 2009 American Express's average ROE was 28%.

[30] This is not a recommendation to buy or sell shares of American Express.

[31] Disclosure: The author does not currently and has never owned shares of American Express.

Summary: Identify quality businesses, those businesses that are not capital-intensive and that have consistently generated strong free cash flows and returns on equity in the past and that have a reasonable expectation of continuing to generate strong cash flows and returns in the future. When these businesses are selling at attractive prices, BUY.

CHAPTER 3: AVERAGING DOWN

A price drop in a good stock is only a tragedy if you sell at that price and never buy more...If you can't convince yourself "When I'm down 25 percent, I'm a buyer" and banish forever the fatal thought "When I'm down 25 percent, I'm a seller," then you'll never make a decent profit in stocks. (Peter Lynch, One Up on Wall Street, *p. 243)*

Averaging down is when you buy a stock at one price, the stock price goes down, and you buy more at the new, reduced price, thereby lowering your average purchase price. This one is a no-brainer. If you understand a business and are excited by its fundamentals at one price, and the fundamentals have not deteriorated, then you should like it more (and buy more) at a lower price.

Let's take a look at a fictional example. Suppose you purchase 100 shares of Incredibleism Company at $20 per share for an investment of $2,000. The next day the stock sells off to $18 per share on the news that the visionary CEO will resign at the end of the year to run for president. You think the market is overreacting, because the company enjoys huge brand loyalty and you believe the CEO has built a culture at the company that will outlive his tenure and that the board will find a suitable replacement. So you buy an additional 100 shares at $18 per share for an investment of $1,800. You now own 200 shares for a total investment of $3,800. By dividing your total investment of $3,800 by the 200 shares you own, you calculate your average cost basis is now $19 per share as opposed to your original purchase price of $20 per share. Averaging down reduced your paper (unrealized) losses from 10% when your cost basis was $20 per share to 5% when your cost basis is $19 per share.[32] In other words, averaging down reduced the amount the stock price now needs to appreciate in order to break even and eventually earn a profit.

Summary: Averaging down is a proven way to boost returns and make money. Enough said.

---

[32] This is called "unrealized" losses because when investing in stocks you don't actually lose money until you sell your shares. In other words, you don't "realize" the losses until you actually sell at a price below your purchase price. Yes, when the stock is trading below your purchase price, your net worth on paper has gone down, but it could just as easily go up the next day if the stock appreciates above your purchase price. You only lock in losses when you sell.

CHAPTER 4: HAVING A BUSINESS OWNER'S MENTALITY

Inactivity strikes us as intelligent behavior. Neither we nor most business managers would dream of feverishly trading highly-profitable subsidiaries because a small move in the Federal Reserve's discount rate was predicted or because some Wall Street pundit has reversed his views on the market. Why, then, should we behave differently with our minority positions [stocks] in wonderful businesses? (Warren Buffett letter to shareholders from 1996)

Most successful investors think of buying stocks as if they are buying the entire business. It doesn't make sense to consistently buy a business one day and sell it the next, and it doesn't make sense to do so with a company's marketable securities either. Think about it: you wouldn't buy a McDonald's franchise one day, sell it the next, and buy it back a month later. That's just silly. Those who take the opposite view trade frequently, jumping in and out of the market monthly, weekly, or even daily, diminishing their returns with high short-term capital gains taxes and trading fees.

Having a business owner's mentality implies more than just having a long-term perspective. It also guides how an investor evaluates a company's investment merit and what information investors should use in the evaluation process. Using a concept I learned from reading Bruce Berkowitz, I evaluate buying shares of a public company just as I would evaluate buying my neighborhood ice cream shop.[33] The ice cream shop has no beta (more on this later), average daily trading volume (the average number of shares that exchange hands daily), or 12-month price target (what an analyst thinks the stock will sell at a year down the road). These metrics are meaningless when buying a private business that you intend to own, operate, and grow over a number of years, and to me, they are meaningless when buying stock in a public company. I am interested in margins, cash flows, management, the competitive landscape, reinvestment and growth opportunities, risks, and, of course, valuation, among other things. What is attractive to the owner of a private business should be attractive to the owner of a portion of a publicly traded business.

And the neat thing about the stock market is that it often lets us become owners at substantially discounted prices. Public markets provide stock investors the opportunity to buy a percentage of a company (through shares of stock) at prices (valuations) at which they normally would not be able to purchase the entire company, because buyouts often require a buyout premium of typically 20% (or higher) above the stock price at the time the deal is announced. Additionally, many of the stocks in the market are highly liquid, meaning that investors can sell shares whenever they want, almost instantly converting stock into cash. But when you own a business outright or invest in a private business (as one of a handful of owners), it can often take longer to find a suitable buyer for your stake, making your investment a lot less liquid. On the flip side, people with money to invest can often find good buying opportunities in the stock market more quickly than they can find the right business to buy in a private market transaction. Business-minded inves-

---

[33] Bruce Berkowitz letter to shareholders from July 2005 available at http://www. fairholmefunds.com/letters (8/28/2013), p. 2.

tors recognize the advantages that public markets provide and take advantage of them.

Summary: As an owner of a stock, you are an owner of a business. Think like one!

CHAPTER 5: HAVING A CONCENTRATED PORTFOLIO

Note: If you do not have the time or desire to research businesses or if you feel you do not have the skills to identify a good investment from a poor one, then you should simply invest in an index fund. Blindly loading up on a few businesses that you know nothing about is a recipe for disaster.

We believe it is preferable to own a small number of companies researched extensively rather than a broad list that could dilute our efforts, focus, and performance. (Bruce Berkowitz letter to shareholders from July 2000, p. 1)

With this quote Bruce Berkowitz is suggesting that when you own more than a handful of stocks, it is terribly difficult to keep tabs on all of them. Successful investing requires adequate research prior to buying and periodic monitoring once you own the stock, but the time and effort you will be able to devote to the research process will decrease as the number of securities you own increases. Additionally, if you own 50 or 100 stocks (or more), you most likely have your capital dispersed thinly across your many holdings. You may, for example, have $10,000 invested in 100 different 1% positions ($100 invested in each of 100 different stocks). It's hard to get rich doing that! If you have $100 invested in a stock and the stock doubles, you now have $200 in that position. This is a great return, but not a lot of money. But if you have $10,000 invested in three stocks ($3,000 in each stock and $1,000 in cash) and one stock doubles, you now have $6,000 invested in that company. This is also a 100% return, but you now have $3,000 additional dollars as opposed to only $100 additional dollars. Successful investors invest a lot of money in their few best ideas, those situations that have limited downside and significant upside.

Taking it a step further, maintaining a concentrated portfolio is almost a necessity if you believe in buying good businesses at discounts to their underlying value, because these opportunities are few and far between. Therefore, when you find a business that meets your criteria, you should buy a considerable chunk of stock. But the flip side is that if you can't find anything worth buying, don't force it. Save your cash for the right buying opportunities. The number of holdings in your portfolio may change throughout your career as opportunities become more or less plentiful, but in general I think owning about 10 high-quality businesses (maybe a few more and maybe a few less) is suitable for those investors with the time and skill to manage their own portfolio.

It is here that investors need to remember that investing decisions should be based on opportunity cost. Before you buy anything, you must compare it to the other opportunities available to you, including increasing your stake in a company you already own. If it is in your portfolio, then presumably you have done extensive research, you understand the business, and you have high conviction about the company's long-term economics and the margin of safety at which you purchased the stock. Buffett urges us to imagine that we are limited to making only 20 investments throughout our investing lifetime. Thinking of portfolio management in this way will force you to buy only the very best opportunities that come across your desk. Most of the time this will be something you have already uncovered, something you already own. Limiting your purchases to only your best ideas implies that the fewer moves you make (i.e., the fewer times you press the buy and sell button), the better your returns will be. "Inactivity" is the mantra of the successful investor.[34]

In Chapter 2 I suggest that if you take only one piece of advice from me, let it be to invest only in companies that have a simple investment thesis. Here is a second piece of advice that I believe equally as strongly in: investing in stocks willy-nilly by taking tiny positions in a bunch of subpar businesses makes no sense. If you're free to buy whatever and whenever you want, why not buy more of a sure thing?[35] Investing should be controlled, reasoned, and decisive. Controlled means you don't buy willy-nilly; you don't buy low-conviction ideas or ideas you have not researched thoroughly. Reasoned means your purchases are based on deep thought and analysis. And decisive means that when your thought and analysis uncovers what you believe to be a great company at a great price, and only then, you invest a significant amount of money.

---

[34] Warren Buffett letter to shareholders from 1996 and Charlie Munger from *Poor Charlie's Almanack*, Expanded Third Edition, p. 102.

[35] In Warren Buffett's letter to shareholders from 1993 he says, "I cannot understand why an investor of that sort elects to put money into a business that is his 20th favorite rather than simply adding that money to his top choices." When Buffett refers to investors "of that sort" he is referring to knowledgeable investors, those who "understand business economics" and competitive positions. This is a crucial point that must not be overlooked. If you understand businesses and can identify a good investment from a risky one, then a concentrated portfolio has the potential to provide above-average returns. But if you do not have the skills to value a business and identify attractive investment opportunities, then a diversified portfolio of stocks is the safest way (and the only way I recommend) for you to participate in the stock market. By far the cheapest way to invest in a diverse portfolio of stocks is to buy an index fund. An index fund will guarantee you market results, which over time have been exceptional. Over the past 50 years, the stock market has returned 10% per year on average.

Summary: Building up big positions in your best ideas is the surest way I know to beat the market and get rich. So, before you buy anything ask yourself if it is worthy of one of your 20 lifetime investments.

CHAPTER 6: WHEN TO SELL

We're partial to putting out large amounts of money where we won't have to make another decision. If you buy something because it's undervalued, then you have to think about selling it when it approaches your calculation of its intrinsic value. That's hard. But, if you can buy a few great companies, then you can sit on your ass. That's a good thing. (*Charlie Munger,* Poor Charlie's Almanack, *Expanded Third Edition, p. 77*)

Many successful investors advocate selling when the market overvalues the stock, management disappoints, or an even more attractive investment opportunity appears and you wish to reallocate the cash. To this I would add, sell when you are wrong. Some indicators you might be wrong are shrinking profits (not from one quarter to the next but over a sustained period of time), new competitors or technologies that emerge and change the competitive landscape, the company's loss of business (market share), or management's destruction of shareholder value by misallocating cash. This list, of course, is incomplete. But just because the stock sells off in the short term does not necessarily mean you are wrong. In fact, if the fundamentals remain strong, this is when you should average down by buying more stock.

I have found that in almost every case where I am wrong, it is because I invested in an industry I did not understand. We should try to expand our circle of competence by reading as much as we can about as many businesses and as many industries as we can.

But until we reach a certain level of competence in a new industry, we should just stick to what we know. For example, before you invest in a 3D printing company, you should understand what additive manufacturing is and how it is taking share from traditional injection molding. You should also understand the competitive landscape (and the growth-by-acquisition model), the possible end markets (including rapid prototyping), the differences between the do-it-yourself (or hobbyist) versus the industrial market, and the risks involved. You should understand the risks of investing in high-growth/high-multiple stocks, the integration risks associated with acquisitions, the risk of paying too much for an acquisition in an industry with a lot of excitement (and therefore high multiples), and the risk that goodwill and intangibles represent a substantial portion of total assets on a company's balance sheet. Additive manufacturing is a very promising technology that allows users to make everything from plastic toys to automobile and airplane parts to medical devices. But unless you understand the science and risks discussed in this paragraph, 3D printing falls outside of your circle of competence. You should read up on it, though; it's pretty exciting stuff.

The other few instances I know I have been wrong occurred when I rushed to buy because I was overjoyed by a recent sell-off in a particular security (and attracted solely to its bargain valuation), without having performed sufficient due diligence beforehand. Each time I make this mistake, I remind myself (too late unfortunately) to always ask "why" a stock is cheap before committing capital. Research should be done prior to buying, not after. In an era when computers are facilitating faster and faster trading, I always try to slow down before I buy anything and ask myself if I can clearly and easily explain why I want to own this business for a long time. If I can't do that, I don't buy. And if I make the mistake of buying a business in which I misjudged the long-term economics or failed to understand as well as I initially thought, I sell.

This chapter was the hardest for me to write because knowing when to sell is so damn hard for me, and that's why buying great businesses that have the ability to increase their underlying value over time is the only way I know how to make money in the stock market. If I buy a great company and pay a little too much, I'll probably still end up OK. But if I buy a company that is losing business and losing money, just because I thought it was cheap, I may end up losing my entire investment as I sit, frozen, contemplating how long I should give this piece of crap company before it "turns itself around." Buy good companies. You'll stress less, sleep better, and preserve your capital, a topic we'll address in the next chapter.

Summary: Knowing when to sell is the hardest aspect of investing, so strive to buy great companies that you are willing to own for a very long time. If you buy the right companies at the right prices, you don't need to worry so much about selling.

CHAPTER 7: PREVENTING PERMANENT LOSS OF CAPITAL

In stocks, we expect every commitment to work out well because we concentrate on conservatively financed businesses [little debt] with strong competitive strengths, run by able and honest people. If we buy into these companies at sensible prices, losses should be rare. (Warren Buffett letter to shareholders from 2002, p. 16)

Warren Buffett has often said that the first rule of investing is to not lose money and the second rule is to never forget rule number one. The reason for this is because risk is the possibility of harm or ruin from the permanent loss of capital, and permanent loss of capital is very hard to recover from.

Perhaps confusingly, minimizing loss is the key to outperforming the market over time. To illustrate, assume you invested $100 and the market goes down 50%. You are now left with $50. But, if the market then rebounds 50%, you are only back to $75, not to your original $100 investment. This is because even though the market recovered 50%, your 50% return is off of a smaller base, $50 versus your original $100 investment. Therefore, if the market is down 50%, you need the market to go back up 100% just to get back to even.

As this quick exercise shows, it's a hell of a lot easier to lose money than it is to make money. Making money takes time. But losing money is quick, and it can be devastating. For this reason, I urge all investors to moderate their return expectations. The stock market has returned about 10% per year on average. Matching the market and earning 10% is not a disaster (it's actually pretty darn good). Losing your entire savings is![36] By avoiding disasters, you're likely to outperform the market by meaningful amounts over an investing career. You should manage risk by investing only in what you know and have researched extensively and buying at a discount to value to insist on a margin of safety. Buying cheap is the surest way to minimize loss, but I have a four-pronged front line of defense I use before I even consider valuation: (1) If I don't understand the business or industry, I don't buy. (2) If the company has too much debt, I don't buy. (3) If the company is losing money (unprofitable), I rarely ever buy. (4) And I have a strict policy against buying on stock tips without first doing adequate research. Trust me when I say you don't want stock tips and you don't need them. Nine out of 10 times the tipster is dead wrong. Use the following dialogue as an example of a situation you want to avoid. My advice if someone approaches you with such a tip is to run (don't walk) away as fast as you can.

Tipster: Dude, you have to buy this stock my friend told me about. He says it's going to the moon.

Successful investor: Thanks for the tip, but I'm happy with the six stocks I own right now. They're all compounding machines and I just don't want to sell them. I have some cash on the sidelines, but I'm just waiting for the right opportunity.

Tipster: This is the right opportunity. This thing is going parabolic.

Successful investor: All right, I'll read up on it. What's the name of the business?

---

[36] Howard Marks does a beautiful job of explaining how to think about returns and how chasing for yield can be dangerous, on p. 213 of *The Most Important Thing Illuminated*. Check it out.

Tipster: I have no idea. All I know is the ticker is CRAPP (a fictional ticker for a fictional business).

Successful investor: You don't know the name? All right, well what do they do?

Tipster: I have no idea what they do. Why does it matter what they do? All you need to know is that the train is leaving the station and you're either on it or you're not. Did I say train? I mean rocket ship, and it's going straight into the stratosphere. My friend told me this stock is a screaming buy. He told me if I want to make bags of money real fast I should buy CRAPP.

Successful investor: Thanks but I don't want to own CRAPP and I've got to run. Bye!!!

I weed out possible stocks by using these four filters before I even attempt to value the business.

Summary: Successful investors spend more time thinking about minimizing loss than they do about making money. When thinking about possible investments, if you find you are seeing only upside potential and no risks, then you are probably not thinking hard enough.

CHAPTER 8: MARKET INEFFICIENCY

I agree that because investors work hard to evaluate every new piece of information, asset prices immediately reflect the consensus view of the information's significance. I do not, however, believe the consensus view is necessarily correct. In January 2000, Yahoo sold at $237. In April 2001 it was at $11. Anyone who argues that the market was right both times has his or her head in the clouds; it has to have been wrong on at least one of those occasions. (Howard Marks, The Most Important Thing, *p. 8)*

Efficient market theory (EMT) says that no one can consistently outperform the market, because each new piece of information (news, press release, earnings report, analyst upgrade or downgrade, etc.) is immediately assimilated and prices immediately adjust to reflect a security's true value. Basically, it says the market is always right and that there are no bargains out there. Although some companies are more accurately priced at times than others (because they receive a lot of Wall Street attention), overall this theory is complete nonsense and is proved flawed year after year as countless investors consistently beat the market. Check out the long-term records of Warren Buffett, Charlie Munger, Bruce Berkowitz, Mario Gabelli, Don Yacktman, Seth Klarman, Peter Lynch, Howard Marks, Michael Burry, Joel Greenblatt, Lou Simpson, and so many more. The numbers don't lie, but the debate rages on.

Summary: Markets are inefficient enough of the time to consistently beat the market and acquire real wealth.

CHAPTER 9: BETA (VOLATILITY) IS NOT A MEASURE OF RISK

For owners of a business – and that's the way we think of shareholders – the academics' definition of risk is far off the mark, so much so that it produces absurdities. (Warren Buffett letter to shareholders from 1993)

Modern portfolio theory says that risk is defined as stock price volatility (how much a stock price moves up or down relative to the market), something referred to as beta. Basically, a stock with a beta of 1 moves just as much as the market when the market moves, and in the same direction. A stock with a beta greater than 1 moves up more than the market when the market moves up and moves down more than the market when the market moves down (i.e., has more volatility). A stock with a beta less than 1 moves up less than the market when the market moves up and moves down less than the market when the market moves down (displays less volatility). Modern portfolio theorists advise "diversifying" away this "risk" by buying a large basket of stocks, in effect just buying the market. This is fine if you want average results.

Volatility is an ignorant and, quite frankly, unfortunate measure of risk, since volatility in stock prices is an investor's best friend. Volatility is what creates opportunities to buy good businesses at attractive prices. Beta theory actually says a stock becomes more risky when its price drops (i.e., when the margin of safety increases), which contradicts the most fundamental tenet of investing, which is to buy low and sell high. The real risk in investing is the risk of losing your money, and you lose money when you pay more than a company is worth or invest in a company that can't easily service its debt.

Summary: Volatility (stock price movements) is the best thing since cheeseburgers and cold beer. Volatility makes successful investing possible; without it there would be no way to buy great stocks at bargain prices.

CHAPTER 10: HAVING A LONG-TERM PERSPECTIVE

Even superior investment strategies may take a long time to show their stuff. If an investment strategy truly makes sense, the longer the time horizon you maintain, the better your chances for ultimate success. Time horizons of 5, 10, or even 20 years are ideal. (Joel Greenblatt, The Little Book That Beats the Market, *p. 94)*

The reasons to be a long-term holder of stocks are numerous: capital gains taxes are lower on long-term holdings; you pay lower trading costs if you aren't constantly jumping in and out of the market; you have the opportunity to build meaningful stakes in great businesses over an investing lifetime; it often takes years for the market price to move up to the underlying business value (and for shareholders to reap rewards); companies with sustainable competitive advantages can actually increase in value over time (a company's value is not set in stone); and the power of compounding interest is a wonderful thing. But compounding takes time to work, so the earlier you start the better (more on this to come later). And last, thinking long term is a defining characteristic of taking a business owner's perspective, and thinking like an owner will greatly improve your chances of success in the stock market.

Summary: Buy a great business and hold on to it.

CHAPTER 11: EMOTIONAL DISCIPLINE

The key to making money in stocks is not to get scared out of them. This point cannot be overemphasized. (Peter Lynch, Beating the Street, *p. 36)*

You need the discipline to not automatically sell when stock prices fall in companies you own, the discipline to not buy when everyone else is buying and the price is expensive, and the discipline to buy a lot when you find a great business selling at an attractive price.

This is the secret ingredient. Emotional discipline is what separates the successful investors from the average and unsuccessful ones. A lot of investors are good at research, modeling, and asking the right questions. But very few investors have the discipline to hold on long enough to allow that research, modeling, and questioning to result in anything. That is, they sell as soon as the stock price dips down. Successful investors are able to ignore what everyone else is saying and what everyone else is doing, meaning they aren't pressured to buy just because the market is buying or to sell just because the market is selling. In other words, successful investors have restraint and patience! Rather than listening to the market, let your research, your estimate of a stock's value, and your convictions determine the best course of action.

Patience (or restraint) and confidence go hand in hand with investing. You must be patient while you sit on your cash, waiting for the right opportunity, and confident to invest a significant amount of your portfolio once that opportunity arises. Then you must be patient again while you wait for the market price to catch up to the business's true value (i.e., while you wait for the market to realize what you have already discovered through your analysis).

Unfortunately, having a temperament suited for investing is the hardest thing to teach, if it can be taught at all. The best this book can do is make you aware of the role that psychology plays in investment success, and to urge you to become aware of your own emotional thresholds and limitations. If you don't think you can deal with large price drops in individual securities, do yourself a favor and just invest in an index fund. Then don't touch that investment, except to periodically add money, until you retire.

Summary: The market is like a roller coaster and you must hold on tight. You'll have days when your portfolio is up and days when your portfolio is down. You'll have days when you feel like you're on top of the world and days when you feel sick to your stomach. Ignore all that nonsense. Do not listen to the market. Let your analysis and valuation of individual stocks determine what you buy and when you sell.

CHAPTER 12: BEING CONTRARIAN

Difficult markets help us succeed as investors...Only in adverse environments do owner-oriented companies with proven records and strong balance sheets sell at bargain prices. (Bruce Berkowitz letter to shareholders from July 2001, p. 1)

A contrarian investor, by definition, is doing the opposite of what the stock market is doing. That is, the contrarian is buying when the market is selling (so prices are falling) and selling when the market is buying (when prices are rising). In fact, contrarianism is the only way to follow the most fundamental principle of investing: to buy low and sell high. As Warren Buffett wrote in his 1997 letter to shareholders and has reminded us on countless occasions since, if you plan to be a "net buyer" of stocks throughout your lifetime, then you should "prefer" falling stock prices. So, my advice is that when the market crashes, if you have money available, you should get to work buying some of the best companies at bargain-basement prices. If you do the opposite and follow the herd, then you are destined for average results at best.

During the recession of 2008-2009, American businesses sunk to their cheapest valuations in a generation. This is when you should have gone all in, buying the best businesses in the world at once-in-a-lifetime bargain prices! But, instead, many investors sold all their holdings, thinking that the world was coming to an end.[37] Selling was a huge mistake. From the market low in March of 2009 to March of 2013, the S&P 500 index has generated a total return (price appreciation plus dividends) of 123% and an annualized return of over 20%.[38] Think about that for a second: 20% annual returns while certificates of deposit are earning less than 1%. The next chapter will show you how 20%, compounded over a number of years, can result in a very large amount of wealth creation.

Summary: The objective is to buy quality companies selling at attractive prices. This is easier to do when the market is selling at 13 or 14 times earnings than when it is selling at 17 or 18 times earnings. Successful investors prefer falling stock prices to rising stock prices so much that falling prices cause giddiness and rising prices cause depression. You can identify true investors by how they react to large swings in the market. If they cash out each time the market falls, or get caught up in the excitement and buy aggressively in a rising market, they don't have a clue. If you have a lifetime of investing ahead of you, you should be depressed when stock prices rise, because it limits your ability to buy the best companies at discount prices.

---

[37] Market crashes can be devastating to some families. The crash of 2008-2009 led to millions of job losses, and losing a job is both physically and emotionally painful. Losing the ability to provide for your family is absolutely gut-wrenching and demoralizing. As unfortunate as it is to sell at a loss during a downturn, I understand that some people have no choice. But many investors who did have a choice (they did not need to sell) still chose to sell out of fear and uncertainty, and this was a mistake.

[38] S&P 500 Return Calculator at http://dqydj.net/sp-500-return-calculator/ (8/28/2013).

CHAPTER 13: THE BEAUTY OF COMPOUNDING INTEREST

Understanding both the power of compound interest and the difficulty of getting it is the heart and soul of understanding a lot of things. (Charlie Munger, Poor Charlie's Almanack, *Expanded Third Edition, p. 74)*

I'll never forget the story my finance professor in business school told us the first day of class, to illustrate the magic of compounding interest. The story goes like this: A king offered to grant a peasant farmer anything he wanted for heroically saving a child from drowning. The king told the farmer he could have a castle, land, or gold or be knighted. Luckily the farmer was an educated man. He asked only that the king place a single grain of wheat on the first square of a chessboard, then two grains on the next square the next day, and four grains on the next square the day after, and so on, until all 64 squares of the chessboard were full. Doubling the number of grains on each successive square means that on the 64th square, the peasant farmer will have 18 quintillion grains of wheat. That's a lot of wheat! If you want to check the math, just use the future value formula ($FV = PV \times (1+r)^t$), where the present value (PV) is 1 because you start with one grain of wheat, the rate (r) is 100% because you are doubling each day, and the number of compounding periods (t) is 64. It turns out that this chessboard illustration of compounding interest is quite popular on the Internet, but the first time I heard it was in business school and it definitely left an impression.

If wheat is not your thing, I'll now try to illustrate the power of compounding interest with money. Assume you make a one-time investment of $10,000 and hold the money in the market for 45 years. If that $10,000 compounds at 10% annually you will end up with about $730,000 at the end of 45 years. Not bad considering you only invested the $10,000 in the first year and never added any new money to the market in the following years. But if your $10,000 compounds at 15% per year for the 45-year period, you will end up with a very nice $5,400,000. If your money compounds at 20% for 45 years, you will end up with nearly $37 million. Boom!!! Now imagine how much you would have if you regularly added to your original $10,000 investment. This illustration shows that even just matching the market's historical 10% annual returns, over a long period of time, is more than enough to acquire a comfortable amount of wealth, and that beating the market by only a few percentage points a year can make you downright filthy rich.[39]

Investing in the stock market is the surest and safest way to accumulate real wealth. Period![40] But to allow the magic of com-

---

[39] I strongly advise against trying to achieve 20% returns. Twenty percent annual returns is what Warren Buffett has achieved over his legendary career. But Warren Buffett very well may be the greatest investor and businessman this world has ever seen. Twenty percent over a long time is very hard to achieve. By striving for 20% you may take the chance of buying a company you do not understand, or that has too much debt, or that everyone else is buying (and is at risk of being too expensive). Doing so is dangerous. Rather, if you decide to manage your own portfolio, I think you should try to match the market or beat it by a point or two. Underperforming the market a year or two now and again is no big deal and it will happen. But if you continue to underperform over a full market cycle (peak to peak), you should consider putting your money in an index fund. With an index fund, you are guaranteed to match the market results for a very low fee.

[40] In the August 2012 issue of *Motley Fool Stock Advisor*, Morgan Housel references a Deutsche Bank Long-Term Asset Return Study that shows that from 1900 to 2010 gold provided average annual returns of 0.58% after inflation, Treasury bonds returned 1.46% after inflation, and stocks returned 6.02% after inflation. Stocks are the far-and-away winner. Investors, at the

pounding to work for you, you must remain substantially invested throughout your life, and because of how the math of compounding works, the earlier you start the better. When I say remain substantially invested I mean investors should not try to time the market. Investors are harmed when they sell simply because the market is falling. This is when they should be buying. But substantially invested does not mean investors should not hold some cash. Indeed, markets are unpredictable and cash allows us to take advantage of opportunities when they become available. I usually keep a minimum of 10% of my portfolio in cash.

In his 2012 letter to shareholders Warren Buffett encourages us to remain invested. He says, "Since the basic game is so favorable, Charlie and I believe it's a terrible mistake to try to dance in and out of it based upon the turn of tarot cards, the predictions of 'experts,' or the ebb and flow of business activity. The risks of being out of the game are huge compared to the risks of being in it."[41]

Summary: Compound interest is the reason to invest. To maximize its power, start early and remain invested throughout your life.

---

very least, should try to maintain the purchasing power of their dollars but should strive to earn returns above and beyond inflation. Inflation is the rate at which prices rise from year to year. Understanding inflation is key to understanding investing, because if you don't understand inflation, you may be confused about what qualifies as a safe investment. Money sitting in a bank earning 1% is anything but safe. You see, inflation is a hungry little animal that feeds on the purchasing power of our dollars. If a savings account is earning 1% and inflation is eating away at 2%, that investor is losing money.

[41] Warren Buffett letter to shareholders from 2012, p. 6.

CHAPTER 14: PREDICTING THE FUTURE VERSUS MONITORING SECULAR TRENDS

We make no attempt to predict how security markets will behave; successfully forecasting short term stock price movements is something we think neither we nor anyone else can do. (Warren Buffett letter to shareholders from 1978)

If Warren Buffett, Charlie Munger, and the other great investors in the world can't predict what markets and economies will do in the near term, neither can you or I or the commentators we hear doing it every single day on TV. This is not to say that you should not pay attention to the world around you. While we don't know which stocks will win or lose in the next week, month, quarter, or year, we can and should pay attention to which industries have long-term secular winds (trends) at their backs, winds that will provide growth opportunities for years if not decades to come. You can spot these trends by reading the news and reading company reports. Once you spot a trend, ask yourself (1) is the trend sustainable? (is it secular in nature or is it just a short-term cyclical thing?) and (2) how can I profit from it? (what businesses will benefit from this trend?)

Here is a list of 10 trends that I am currently keeping an eye on.

   (1) Because of new drilling technologies used to reach hard-to-access oil and gas like horizontal drilling and hydraulic

fracturing, North America could be on its way to energy independence.

(2) Americans are living longer, but we are becoming more obese and more diseased. Diabetes has become an epidemic and is afflicting children at an alarming rate.[42] The Centers for Disease Control and Prevention estimates that 1 in 3 Americans could have diabetes by 2050.[43]

(3) The U.S. population is aging. Ten thousand baby boomers turn 65 years old every day in the U.S.[44]

(4) Feeding the exploding population around the world will be a challenge.

(5) More than half of the population growth in the United States is coming from Hispanics.[45]

(6) Eighty-five percent of the global population (and 50% of the U.S.) still pays with paper (cash or check), but credit cards, debit cards, and other forms of electronic payments are gaining share.[46]

(7) The middle class is growing in emerging markets. With more disposable income, they will demand more goods and services like cars, fuel to power their cars, beef and other

---

[42] The statistics on childhood diabetes are absolutely horrifying, and I believe we must do something about it. If you want to read more, please see http://www.diabetes.org/for-media/2012/sci-sessions-SEARCH.html (9/10/2013) and http://www.diabetes.org/for-media/2012/number-of-youth-with-diabetes-projected-to-rise-by-2050.html (9/10/2013). For statistics on diabetes in general, please see http://www.diabetes.org/assets/pdfs/misc-research-documents/case-for-research_2012_1.pdf (9/10/2013).

[43] "Number of Americans with Diabetes Projected to Double or Triple by 2050," available at http://www.cdc.gov/media/pressrel/2010/r101022.html (9/27/2013).

[44] Pew Research Center article "Baby Boomers Retire," available at http://www.pewresearch.org/daily-number/baby-boomers-retire/ (9/6/2013).

[45] Ceasar, Stephen. "Hispanic Population Tops 50 Million in U.S.," available at http://articles.latimes.com/2011/mar/24/nation/la-na-census-hispanic-20110325 (9/25/2013).

[46] MasterCard 2010 annual report, p. 4, available at http://investorrelations.mastercardintl.com/phoenix.zhtml?c=148835&p=irol-reportsannual (9/13/2013).

proteins, candy and other snacks, TV and Internet access, smartphones, and alcoholic beverages.

(8) Americans are drinking more wine and liquor and less beer. But craft and import beers are experiencing faster growth than the overall U.S. beer market.

(9) The world is buying more and more goods online. This is a threat to some brick-and-mortar stores, but could also be an opportunity for others such as package delivery companies (someone has to deliver all those packages purchased over the Internet), payment processing companies (like Visa and MasterCard), credit card companies (like American Express and Discover), and other e-commerce companies (like eBay's PayPal) because you can't pay with cash online.

(10) More and more consumers are starting to stream video (both television shows and movies) over the Internet, allowing them to watch what they want, when they want, on whatever device they want (TV, smartphone, tablet, etc.) and as much as they want (binge on an entire season of a popular TV show during a weekend).

Remember, your job is to ask how sustainable is the trend and which businesses will a particular trend benefit and which will it harm. I will now attempt to answer both questions, using a few of the trends as examples.

From years of research, I believe that global population growth will put major strains on the global food supply. The global population is expected to grow by two billion people by 2050, yet already a child dies of hunger every 11 seconds. One industry expert even believes the world will have to produce more food in the next 40 years than it did in the previous 10,000 years.[47] So I think this trend is both troublesome and long-term. Now, that I've answered question one, my next job is to research the different companies that I think can make money off the trend. One possible company is CF Industries.[48]

CF is North America's largest nitrogen fertilizer producer. Nitrogen is one of three primary fertilizers used in farming. The other two are potash and phosphate. The world will need more of all three types of fertilizers as it struggles to feed the growing population. More mouths to feed will mean more demand for CF's products. CF can also grow by taking market share from imports. North America currently imports about 40% of its nitrogen fertilizer. As CF adds capacity (builds new production facilities) and increases its output, it should be able to supply additional fertilizer to North American farmers, reducing the farmers' need to rely on imports. Additionally, CF currently has a cost advantage because natural gas accounts for about 70% of the cash cost to produce nitrogen. Natural gas prices are unusually low in North America right now (and about 3x-4x lower than natural gas prices in Europe and Asia), meaning that CF's primary input cost (raw material) is exceptionally cheap. Low raw material costs have translated into very strong earnings and cash flows.[49] Over the past five years, CF has averaged a little over $1 billion in annual free cash flow generation

---

[47] Weiss, Kenneth R. "Beyond 7 Billion: The Biggest Generation," available at http://www.latimes.com/news/nationworld/world/population/la-fg-population-matters1-20120722-html,0,7213271.htmlstory (9/18/2013) and Weiss, Kenneth R. "Beyond 7 Billion: Hunger Without End," available at http://www.latimes.com/news/nationworld/world/population/la-fg-population-matters3-20120726-html,0,2752228.htmlstory (9/18/2013).

[48] Disclosure: the author does not currently and has never owned shares of CF Industries.

[49] Research for CF Industries comes from years of reading company filings and investor presentations, which are available at http://phx.corporate-ir.net/phoenix.zhtml?c=190537&p =irol-presentations (9/4/2013).

and 30% returns on equity. It currently trades at about 11x FCF and 2x book value.

But of course there are risks. Remember to always ask what can go wrong. The biggest risk is a rise in natural gas prices. If natural gas prices go up, CF's expenses will go up, which will crimp earnings and cash flows. This is a real concern, considering natural gas prices are rebounding off historic lows and that the United States is exploring new uses for its abundant supply of natural gas, including building new manufacturing facilities that will use natural gas as both a feed stock and fuel source, increasing the use of natural gas as a transportation fuel, and possibly exporting natural gas to take advantage of high selling prices abroad. Other risks include adverse weather conditions (example: drought) or a drop in the price of corn (which is a major crop in the U.S.), which would decrease the demand for fertilizers, or a significant decrease in the price of potash or phosphate fertilizers, which may cause farmers to use more phosphate and potash and less nitrogen. But I'm not so worried about occasional adverse weather or an occasional poor harvest, because I am confident that the long-term demand for fertilizers will grow as the population grows. I'm also not so worried about one fertilizer taking share from another, because I think the world will need more of all three fertilizers, and CF sells both nitrogen and phosphate-based fertilizers. Furthermore, these fertilizers are used to grow crops that are then used in animal feed (to feed cattle and chickens, etc.), and the livestock are needed to satisfy the increasing demand for protein in developing countries. Although I am not overly concerned about occasional adverse weather, I think a major risk is dramatic climate change that drastically changes temperatures or weather patterns around the world, increases the number or severity of storms, or causes decade-long draughts. Dramatic climate change could ruin harvests and decrease the demand for fertilizers.[50]

For my second example, I am going to combine two trends: the increased oil and natural gas production in North America and the growing demand for fuel around the world. There are lots of ways to play the oil and gas industry, such as investing in exploration and production companies (those companies that drill for oil and own the reserves), refineries (those companies that refine crude oil into gasoline, diesel, and other products), and pipelines (those companies that own the pipes and charge a toll for moving the oil from the well to the refineries). But for this example I will discuss an oil and gas services company.

National Oilwell Varco manufactures and sells rig systems and mechanical components and supplies used for both land and off-shore drilling rigs around the world.[51] National Oilwell Varco is the largest supplier of these rig parts in the world, with over 50% share of the global market. The stock has been selling off recently because, due to cheap natural gas prices, there has been a slowdown in onshore North American drilling. But with so much attention on the North American shale boom, some investors overlook that off-shore drilling in the Gulf of Mexico is growing, as is drilling internationally. National Oilwell Varco will also benefit from the growth of floating, production, storage, and offloading (FPSO) vessels and the possibility of increased shale drilling abroad, which today re-

---

[50] This is not a recommendation to buy or sell CF Industries. I am just trying to demonstrate the importance of keeping an eye on major trends and I used CF as an example of one of many possible ways to invest in that trend. The analysis that I provide on CF is incomplete and is not a recommendation to take action. But this analysis can serve as a snapshot of the analysis that is necessary to understand a business and the industry it operates in.

[51] Disclosure: the author owns shares of National Oilwell Varco.

mains in its infancy.[52] The shale revolution is actually just getting started. Although the United States has a supposed 100-year supply of natural gas, China, Argentina, and Algeria all have larger shale reserves than the U.S. (but shale drilling abroad has barely started).[53] National Oilwell recently reported a record backlog of almost $14 billion (backlog is a measure of future business) and management expressed confidence in its balance sheet and future cash flows by doubling the quarterly dividend (that's a 100% increase in the dividend).[54] National Oilwell Varco has averaged about 13% ROE over the past five years and currently trades at about 29x FCF and 1.5x book value.

One of the biggest risks for National Oilwell is a sustained drop in the price of oil (and natural gas, to a lesser extent). When the price of oil drops, exploration and production companies cut their capital budgets and drill for less oil. Fewer rigs operating around the world will mean less demand for National Oilwell Varco's parts and services. Other major risks include a rapid adoption of alternative sources of energy (like wind and solar) that replace demand for fossil fuels or if one of National Oilwell's parts fails and is responsible for a major oil spill or deadly explosion, similar to the Macondo well explosion in the Gulf of Mexico in 2010.[55] Furthermore, the future of shale drilling is uncertain. For one, hydraulic fracturing

---

[52] Research for National Oilwell came from years of reading company filings, a premium (members only) report from The Motley Fool, and other commentary from The Motley Fool such as http://www.fool.com/investing/general/2013/05/25/3-stock-tips-you-cant-live-without.aspx (9/4/2013).

[53] Spegele, Brian, and Scheck, Justin. "Energy-Hungry China Struggles to Join Shale-Gas Revolution," available at http://online.wsj.com/article/SB10001424127887323980604579030883246871124.html (9/6/2013).

[54] National Oilwell Varco second quarter 2013 earnings press release available at http://finance.yahoo.com/news/national-oilwell-varco-announces-time-110000764.html (9/13/2013).

[55] A National Oilwell Varco part was in no way involved in the Macondo well disaster. I am just listing examples of possible risks.

requires immense amounts of water, but water is in short supply in many parts of the world (especially in China). Global populations, already thirsting for water, may protest the use of water for drilling. Also, there are currently studies under way to determine if the fracking fluids (chemicals) used to break up shale rock formations pollute underground water supplies. Shale formations are below the water table, but any conclusive evidence that hydraulic fracturing is polluting drinking water could put a quick stop to the drilling. Of course, large energy companies have lots of money to spend on research and development, and new technologies could possibly be developed to protect the water should contamination prove to be a real problem. Nevertheless, governments around the world may decide to restrict fracking for one reason or another, whether it be water or other environmental concerns, population density near drilling sites, or another reason entirely. Yet another risk is that National Oilwell Varco may have missed a major opportunity to establish a presence in the subsea (deep sea blowout preventers and robots working to build and repair oil drilling infrastructure on the sea floor) market for parts and services.[56] Two of National Oilwell's competitors recently formed a joint venture to take a substantial lead in subsea services, a very promising frontier as offshore drilling is focusing more and more on reserves in ultra-deep waters.[57]

MasterCard and Visa are positioned to profit from three of the long-term trends I mentioned earlier: (1) the movement away

---

[56] Caplinger, Dan. "Will National Oilwell Varco Earnings Stall Out?" available at http://www.fool.com/investing/general/2013/07/26/will-national-oilwell-varco-earnings-stall-out.aspx (9/6/2013).

[57] This is not a recommendation to buy or sell National Oilwell Varco. I am just trying to demonstrate the importance of keeping an eye on major trends and I used National Oilwell as an example of one of many possible ways to invest in that trend. The analysis that I provide on National Oilwell is incomplete and is not a recommendation to take action. But this analysis can serve as a snapshot of the analysis that is necessary to understand a business and the industry it operates in.

from paying with paper, (2) the growth of online shopping, and (3) the continued growth of the middle class in emerging markets.[58] MasterCard and Visa also have two competitive advantages. They both have strong, trusted brands, and both benefit from network effects. Network effects means that the more people with MasterCard and Visa branded cards will encourage more merchants (stores) to accept MasterCard and Visa and the more merchants that accept their cards, the more consumers will be encouraged to obtain one (or both). Unlike credit card companies that issue credit to consumers and businesses, Visa and MasterCard do not face default risk. Rather, Visa and MasterCard earn fees to process credit and debit card transactions on their respective networks. These fees provide stable and strong free cash flows and because their business models are not capital-intensive, Visa and MasterCard can operate with very little (or even zero) debt.[59]

But Visa and MasterCard also face considerable risks. First, they are facing fierce competition from players like eBay's PayPal, Google, possibly Facebook and Apple, and numerous startups (like Square) entering the payments industry. PayPal has become the preferred method of payment for many online shoppers and is now aggressively expanding into brick-and-mortar stores, but PayPal also accepts Visa and MasterCard on its platform, so only time will tell how this competitive dynamic plays out. Nevertheless, MasterCard (and Visa may follow) is trying to defend its competitive position by charging additional fees on digital wallets such

---

[58] Disclosure: the author owns shares of Visa. The author does not currently and has never owned shares of MasterCard.

[59] This is not a recommendation to buy or sell Visa or MasterCard. I am just using them to help explain the payments industry and as one of many possible ways to invest in the industry. The analysis that I provide on Visa and MasterCard is incomplete and is not a recommendation to take action. But this analysis can serve as a snapshot of the analysis that is necessary to understand a business and the industry it operates in.

as PayPal, Google Wallet, and Square.[60] MasterCard and Visa also have multiple mobile initiatives under way to ensure they are not left out of the mobile payments revolution. In fact, both Visa and MasterCard have launched their own mobile wallets and have joined the mobile-wallet consortium, Isis, which was created by Verizon, AT&T, and T-Mobile.[61] As with all technology companies, Visa and MasterCard must continue to innovate and stay at the forefront of consumer trends. Otherwise they risk technological obsolescence.

Perhaps the more serious threats are government regulation and litigation. Regulators in the U.S. and around the world are seeking to limit the interchange fees that card-issuing banks charge merchants each time a customer pays with a debit card. Banks receive these fees, but they also pay other fees to Visa and MasterCard to process credit and debit card transactions. Although interchange fees are revenues received by banks, Visa and MasterCard fear that if banks are receiving less revenue in the form of lower interchange fees, then the banks will seek to pay lower fees to the payment processors to offset lost revenues from debit card transactions. On the litigation front, Visa and MasterCard recently agreed to pay about $7 billion to settle a class action lawsuit arguing that Visa and MasterCard conspired to set interchange fees at "arbitrarily high levels." But many large retailers (merchants) are trying to get the

---

[60] Barr, Alistair. "EBay Hit as 'Gloves Come Off' Over PayPal Digital Wallet Fee," available at http://www.reuters.com/article/2013/03/18/net-us-ebay-paypal-fee-idUSBRE92H0W320130318 (9/24/2013).

[61] "War of the Virtual Wallets," available at http://www.economist.com/news/finance-and-economics/21566644-visa-mastercard-and-other-big-payment-networks-need-not-be-victims-shift (9/24/2013) and Wester, James "Visa, MasterCard, Amex and Discover to Join Isis," available at http://www.mobilepaymentstoday.com/article/182643/Visa-MasterCard-Amex-and-Discover-to-join-Isis (9/24/2013).

settlement overturned because the settlement would prevent future action being taken against Visa and MasterCard.[62]

I could discuss companies with exposure to each trend, but in my quest to keep this book short, the final trend I will discuss is the frightening growth of diabetes. There are a few primary players in the insulin market, but I will analyze Novo Nordisk because it is the largest.[63] Novo Nordisk, a Danish company, is the world leader in diabetes care, with 50% share of the global insulin market. Novo also sells insulin delivery products like insulin pens. Novo's growth will come from the growing population of diabetics and innovation and development of new drugs. Novo is also currently trying to get an existing diabetes drug approved to treat obesity in people with Type 2 diabetes. Having one drug that can both control insulin levels and help with weight loss could prove to be a large revenue generator.[64] Additionally, many diabetic patients are switching from human insulin to modern insulin medications. This is good for Novo because it offers both, but modern insulin is safer and controls blood sugar levels better, so it is priced higher and provides higher profit margins.[65]

Novo Nordisk's strategy is to focus intensely on only a few diseases so that it can become the global leader in the space. In addition to its diabetes products, Novo Nordisk is also a leader in hemophilia and other rare bleeding disorders, as well as the global

---

[62] Johnson, Andrew R. "Merchants Square Off With Visa and MasterCard Over Swipe-Fee Settlement," available at http://blogs.wsj.com/moneybeat/2013/09/12/merchants-square-off-with-visa-mastercard-over-swipe-fee-settlement/ (9/23/2013).

[63] Disclosure: The author does not currently and has never owned shares of Novo Nordisk.

[64] Macaluso, Max. "Is This an Obesity-Drug Success or Failure?" available at http://www.fool.com/investing/general/2013/03/18/is-this-an-obesity-drug-success-or-failure.aspx?source=isesitlnk0000001&mrr=1.00 (9/23/2013).

[65] Source: June 2013 issue of *Morningstar StockInvestor* newsletter.

leader in growth hormone, with 24% market share.[66] Novo also has drugs in early-stage trials to treat autoimmune and inflammatory diseases such as rheumatoid arthritis, lupus, and Crohn's disease.[67]

The pharmaceutical industry provides certain barriers to entry, making it difficult (but not impossible) for new companies to enter the market and pose a significant challenge to the established players. For one, research and development and clinical trials are long (sometimes taking more than 10 years), expensive processes, and once a drug is approved and patented, its profits are protected for up to 20 years. Also, Novo (like all global pharmaceutical companies) has manufacturing and distribution facilities strategically located around the world so that it can meet local demand and reduce production and shipping costs. These facilities are expensive and take time to build, further deterring new competitors from entering the market. Furthermore, the diabetes industry has the added benefit of very loyal patients. Once diabetics find a drug that is well-tolerated by the body and that allows them to live a comfortable life, they stick with it. According to Morningstar, "Diabetes is a chronic disease, and diabetics are extremely sticky customers: About 95% of patients stay on their current therapy from year to year."[68] Novo Nordisk's strategy of being the global leader in treating only a few diseases, the competitive advantages provided by patents and a global supply chain, and unique characteristics of the diabetes industry have provided Novo with robust and growing

---

[66] Novo Nordisk 2012 Annual Report, p. 8, available at http://novonordisk.com/images/annual_report/2012/Novo-Nordisk-AR-2012-en.pdf (9/24/2013).

[67] Novo Nordisk 2012 Annual Report, p. 11.

[68] Source: August 2013 issue of *Morningstar StockInvestor* newsletter, p. 28, available to members at http://msi.morningstar.com/.

free cash flows, a five-year average free cash flow margin of 25%, and a five-year average return on equity of 40%.[69]

Novo Nordisk investors are currently concerned because two of their promising new insulin drugs need to undergo additional cardiovascular safety trials before being approved by the FDA. Although these two drugs have been approved in some countries outside of the United States, this may delay their launch in the U.S. until 2016.[70] Further delays or an adverse outcome to the cardiovascular trials would represent a significant setback. Novo experienced another recent setback when Express Scripts (the largest U.S. pharmacy benefits manager) ended its contract with Novo, replacing Novo's diabetes medications with medications from Eli Lilly and other competitors.[71]

Novo faces other risks as well. Patents represent both a competitive advantage and a risk for drug companies. Patents ensure high prices and protect profits for about 20 years, but when patents on blockbuster drugs expire, companies risk losing a major source of revenue (because generic drug manufacturers put out low-cost generics) and its margins and cash flows will suffer. Novo Nordisk has some years before its major patents expire, and it currently has a strong pipeline of diabetes drugs to replace drugs that go off-patent (examples include long-lasting insulins that don't need to be injected daily and oral insulins). Novo has a long history of innovation, but should it ever shift its focus away from research and development, it would be cause for concern. Pharmaceutical companies

---

[69] Source: Morningstar.

[70] Source: August 2013 issue of *Morningstar StockInvestor* newsletter.

[71] Schwartzkopff, Frances. "Novo Falls as U.S. Contract Loss Fuels Concern: Copenhagen Mover," available at http://www.bloomberg.com/news/2013-09-03/novo-falls-as-u-s-contract-loss-fuels-concern-copenhagen-mover.html (9/27/2013).

must remain on the cutting-edge of drug science and technology or risk product obsolescence.

Barriers to entry in the pharmaceutical industry are high, but not insurmountable and new competition presents an additional risk. At least one smaller company has gained significant attention by developing an inhalable insulin product that is now in late-stage trials. All else being equal, patients would prefer to inhale their medications as opposed to injecting them.[72] But smaller pharmaceutical companies sometimes choose to partner with a big pharma company to help bring the product to market on a mass scale (by using the larger company's sales and marketing team and distribution network). If this smaller company chooses to partner with one of Novo's competitors, it presents a risk. If it chooses to partner with Novo, it could present an opportunity.[73] Research-driven pharmaceutical companies also need to retain and acquire top talent. If some of Novo's top scientists decide to go work for these smaller, more exciting biotechnology companies, it would be disruptive and could possibly hinder new drug development.

Government legislation is yet another risk. I am unsure how healthcare reform (Obamacare) in the United States will affect pharmaceutical companies, and austerity measures (spending cuts and tax increases) around the world are making it difficult for patients and governments to pay premium prices for the best medications. Lower government reimbursement rates mean that patients may have to pay more out-of-pocket costs for their prescriptions at a time when consumers have less money in their pockets because of stagnant wages, higher healthcare costs, and for some people,

---

[72] Macaluso, Max. "Is the Price Right for Novo Nordisk?" available at http://www.fool.com/investing/general/2013/02/21/is-the-price-right-for-novo-nordisk.aspx (9/23/2013).

[73] Speights, Keith. "The Coming Diabetes Wars," available at http://www.fool.com/investing/general/2013/05/23/the-coming-diabetes-wars.aspx (9/23/2013).

higher taxes. A final concern for pharmaceutical companies in general are possible side effects from future drugs (sometimes side effects don't show up in clinical trials because they develop only with long-term use) that can damage the company's credibility and lead to possible lawsuits and product recalls.[74]

In addition to monitoring trends, you should be aware of the overall psychology (mood) of the stock market. In *The Most Important Thing*, Howard Marks provides a great checklist for "taking the temperature of the market" on page 131. This checklist will help you form an opinion about whether markets are getting riskier (more expensive) and remind you to remain ever vigilant, but it should not be used to "time" when you should be in or out of the market. As we learned in the previous chapter, we should remain substantially invested, buying and selling based on valuation of the individual securities in our portfolios and constantly searching for investments in the cheaper parts of the market.

One other thing: Successful investors have a deep understanding and appreciation for history. They understand that recessions come and go, cycles shift from peak to trough and back again, and unexpected, damaging shocks will occur from time to time, but the stock market, over a long period of time, will continue to reach new highs. Since 1928 the stock market has dropped 20% about once every four years and has crashed 30% about once every decade. The market gets cut in half about two to three times per century.[75]

---

[74] This is not a recommendation to buy or sell Novo Nordisk. I am just trying to demonstrate the importance of keeping an eye on major trends and I used Novo Nordisk as an example of one of many possible ways to invest in that trend. The analysis that I provide on Novo Nordisk is incomplete and is not a recommendation to take action. But this analysis can serve as a snapshot of the analysis that is necessary to understand a business and the industry it operates in.

[75] Housel, Morgan. "What I Plan to Do When the Market Crashes," available at http://www.fool.com/investing/general/2013/08/19/what-i-plan-to-do-when-the-market-crashes.aspx?source=isesitlnk0000001&mrr=1.00 (9/10/2013).

But the pullbacks are only temporary, presenting true investors an opportunity to buy businesses with large competitive advantages at fire-sale prices, before the market recovers and shoots past its previous high. The market will continue to expand as businesses innovate and grow, new businesses are formed, and investors look to the stock market as the surest way to grow wealth and protect against inflation.

Summary: There are three important takeaways from this chapter. First, if someone tells you they know what a company's stock price will be down the road, the person is either lying or out of his mind. You should simply aim to buy good businesses that will do well over the next 10, 20, 30 years, or longer. Second, pay attention to long-term trends. Third, the market will definitely nose-dive again at some point. You should see this as an opportunity, not as a threat.

CHAPTER 15: THE RESEARCH AND DUE DILIGENCE PROCESS

We're light on financial yardsticks; we apply lots of subjective criteria: Can we trust management? Can it harm our reputation? What can go wrong? Do we understand the business? Does it require capital infusions to keep it going? What is the expected cash flow? We don't expect linear growth; cyclicality is fine with us as long as the price is appropriate. (Charlie Munger, Poor Charlie's Almanack, *Expanded Third Edition, p. 219)*

Just like a business owner will have a deep understanding of his business, you should strive to have a keen grasp of the stocks you own and the industries they operate in. You do this by reading their annual and quarterly reports, the reports of their competitors, and industry and trade reports. And read newspapers, lots of them. Newspapers are a good place to source ideas, expand your circle of competence (expand the number of industries you understand), keep up with current events, and take the temperature of the market, as we discussed in the previous chapter. If you don't love to read or don't have the time, you should probably just invest in an index fund, which will guarantee you market (average) results with very low fees.

The research process is about reading, asking questions, and trying to disprove your own thesis. Here are seven questions that I ask before I buy any business: (1) Are the fundamentals strong and/or trending up (this is when I perform financial statement analysis and look at the various ratios and metrics)? (2) Do I think this company will be around in 50 years (i.e., does it have a sustainable competitive advantage?)? (3) How will competition from the Internet affect the company? (4) What are the risks (i.e., what could go wrong?)? (5) What is its record of capital allocation (what are its priorities for cash?)? (6) Is the business selling at an attractive price? and (7) If the stock is cheap, why? Always ask why!!!

All seven questions are crucial, but I want to take a moment to focus on the capital allocation question because it is so terribly important if you plan to be a long-term investor in equities, yet it is highly misunderstood or neglected. Quite simply, a CEO's primary job is capital allocation. Good CEOs allocate capital in ways that increase shareholder value, and bad CEOs don't know the first thing about capital allocation, often destroying shareholder value by paying too much for acquisitions (and eventually having to write down the goodwill acquired in the purchase) or buying back stock at prices above the underlying business value.

Free cash flow can be used to reinvest back in the business (for example, opening new stores), buy back stock, pay dividends, make acquisitions, or pay down debt, or it can just build up on the balance sheet. Each of the above uses of cash can benefit shareholders when done properly. But poor management decisions with owners' earnings can also be catastrophic. If the stock is not priced attractively to warrant buybacks, and if management can't reinvest the capital at above-average returns, then management should simply return the excess cash to shareholders in the form of a dividend. Warren Buffett makes this point as clear as a crystal when he says, "[Y]ou should wish your earnings to be reinvested if they can be expected to earn high returns, and you should wish them paid to you if low returns are the likely outcome of reinvestment."[76]

If capital allocation is still a bit confusing to you, here is a short primer. Capital allocation, just like most everything in finance, is about buying low and selling high. Therefore, if a company buys back its own stock, it should do so cheaply. If a company makes an acquisition, it should do so cheaply. If a company uses its own stock as a currency to buy another company (so it is selling stock in this case), it should do so only when its stock is fairly valued or expensive in order to avoid overly diluting existing shareholders.[77] If a business can't find anything better to do with excess capital, it should pay a dividend. It's all very basic, yet so many CEOs mess it up. If you think I'm being harsh on CEOs, consider this: "[I]n the third quarter of 2007, when share prices were near their peak, members of the S&P 500-stock index spent $171 billion on buybacks. In the first quarter of 2009, with the market near its low, they spent just $31 billion."[78] If this isn't ass-backward, I don't know what is. For a more comprehensive review of capital allocation, I highly encourage you to read *The Outsiders* by William Thorndike, perhaps the greatest book on business and management I have ever read.

I have one last suggestion, which is to ask yourself this question: if you could own only one company, which would it be? Owning only one stock is not advisable for most investors, but asking this question is an effective thought exercise because it forces investors to think like

---

[76] Warren Buffett letter to shareholders from 1984.

[77] To understand dilution, assume a company wants to raise $100 by selling stock. If the current stock price is $1, then the company needs to issue 100 new shares. But if the current stock price is $100, then it only needs to issue one new share. Each new share issued dilutes the earnings per share for existing shareholders, so the fewer new shares issued the better. And the way to issue fewest shares is to do so when the stock is priced higher rather than lower.

[78] Arends, Brett. "How to Tell When a Stock Buyback Is Good for Investors," available at http://online.wsj.com/article/SB10001424127887324731304578193352546252328.html (8/30/2013).

an owner (and not like a trader), forces investors to intensely study the industry and the business's competitive position within the industry (and the sustainability of that position), and encourages investors to buy only what they understand and admire.

Before summarizing this chapter, I want to say a few words about dividends. I am not strictly an income investor, meaning I do not limit my stock purchases to only those companies that pay a dividend. Although I study a company's dividend policy, dividends are not one of my primary investing criteria. That being said, I really do like dividends: if I find a business with a long-term competitive advantage selling at an attractive price, a healthy dividend just makes the story that much better. If you remember what I said in Appendix 1, a company's net income (earnings) belongs exclusively to shareholders (owners of the company). The company can distribute the earnings to shareholders in the form of a dividend or retain the earnings to fund future growth (the earnings that are plowed back into the company's coffers are called retained earnings). When a company decides to pay a dividend, it typically pays out a percentage of earnings (say 20% or 30%) and retains the rest. This dividend payout ratio (the percentage of earnings paid out) is calculated as the annual dividend per share divided by the earnings per share. The dividend yield (the dividend relative to the stock price) is calculated as the annual dividend per share divided by the stock price per share. In general, fast-growth companies do not pay dividends, because they reinvest every last dime into things like research and development, employee training, and marketing. More mature companies that have strong balance sheets, stable earnings, and fewer growth opportunities often pay out a percentage of earnings to shareholders. I like dividends because (1) they are a sign that management (and the board of directors) has confidence in the balance sheet and future earnings of the business, (2) they indicate a shareholder-friendly management team, (3) if a company has committed to paying a common stock dividend, it has less money available to waste on potentially value-destroying acquisitions, (4) reinvested dividends can compound wealth at a very satisfactory rate, and (5) the dividend yield gives investors a base off of which to estimate expected annual returns. With regard to point number 5, as an example, if I assume that Coca-Cola will grow earnings per share at about 5% per year and the current dividend yield is 3%, then I expect Coca-Cola stock to return about 8% per year. I can then use this 8% figure to compare the attractiveness of Coca-Cola to other opportunities available in the market. When analyzing a company's dividend, you should look at the company's history of increasing the dividend from year to year, the company's ability to increase the dividend going forward, and the safety of the dividend (does the company have the finances to maintain the dividend in a tough economic environment?).

Summary: If you cannot confidently answer the seven questions posed in this chapter, you should not buy the stock. Period!!!

CHAPTER 16: DEBT

More than anything else, it's debt that determines which companies will survive and which will go bankrupt in a crisis. (Peter Lynch, One Up on Wall Street, *p. 202)*

Warren Buffett once advised me in a letter: "John, don't borrow money. It works 99% of the time and kills you the other 1%. You'll do fine without it." I heed Warren's advice and I hope you do too. Debt is explosive and I personally avoid investing on margin (borrowing against my stock portfolio) and avoid investing in companies with excessive debt. Which begs the question, what qualifies as too much debt on a company's balance sheet?

Appropriate debt levels will vary depending on the industry, but here are a few guidelines I use when analyzing a company's balance sheet.

Preferably, I try to find businesses that have zero debt. In my opinion, all else being equal, a company that can pay its bills and generate juicy profits without debt is better than a company that requires leverage to achieve the same things. But a company can have debt and still have a rock-solid balance sheet. So, the next thing I look for is a company with a net cash position, meaning they have more cash on the balance sheet than long-term debt (or you can use total debt). Simply subtract long-term debt (or total debt) from cash to get net cash. But if a company has more debt than cash, then it has a net debt position, something that I don't like to see.

Then, I examine the leverage ratios. I focus on companies that have a debt-to-equity (debt divided by shareholders' equity) of 0.5 (50%) or less, indicating the company has at least two times more equity than debt. Finally, I usually feel comfortable with a company that has a long-term debt-to-total-capital ratio of no more than 35%. I calculate this ratio as LTD/(LTD plus shareholders' equity). There is a lot more to evaluating a company's financial strength, like looking at liquidity ratios (example: current assets/current liabilities of at least 1x and preferably 2x) and the interest coverage ratio (EBIT/interest expense), which I will discuss in more detail in Appendix 2.

Summary: Avoid margin debt (don't borrow to buy stocks) and investing in companies with too much debt.

CHAPTER 17: PUTTING THE PRINCIPLES TOGETHER

Our investments continue to be few in number and simple in concept: The truly big investment idea can usually be explained in a short paragraph. (Warren Buffett letter to shareholders from 1994)

Human nature makes investing successfully very difficult. Often emotions, not logic, steer our decision making. Although investing successfully is quite difficult, I think finding intelligent investments is a relatively simple process, even if it takes lots of time and effort. I have tried to stick with this theme of simplicity by discussing only a handful of metrics to evaluate businesses: FCF margin, FCF yield, return on equity (ROE), return on invested capital (ROIC), net cash, debt/equity, and LTD/total capital. Good businesses are those that generate strong cash flows and high returns of capital. Beyond that, I choose to focus on cash on hand, debt-to-equity, and long-term debt to total capital to shed some light on understanding the balance sheet. There are tons more metrics investors focus on, such as liquidity ratios, other debt ratios, profit margins, other cash flow measures, coverage ratios, turnover ratios, and other valuation ratios, and the list goes on. Performing an exhaustive analysis is helpful, but focusing on the few ratios discussed in this book, and understanding what the numbers mean, will help guide your search for intelligent long-term investments.

If you have made it this far, then you are ready for a curveball: the metrics discussed in this book apply better to certain industries than to others. They are appropriate for evaluating most consumer-oriented, manufacturing, and distribution businesses. Evaluating financial service companies, however, requires looking at some ratios we have not discussed (and will not discuss in this book). For example, when evaluating banks, investors often examine net interest income, net interest margin, noninterest income, return on assets, the asset/equity ratio, the efficiency ratio, loan loss reserves as a percentage of total loans, the loan-to-deposit ratio, certificates of deposit as a percentage of total deposits, and price-to-tangible book value (P/TBV is discussed in Appendix 1). The measures we discussed have a place in bank analysis as well. Return on equity is a crucial measure of bank performance, and price-to-earnings and price-to-book ratios (both explained in Appendix 1) are helpful measures of relative value.

Insurance companies require yet a different set of metrics. Insurance investors focus on things like premiums, float, losses and loss adjustment expenses, loss ratios, expense ratios, combined ratios, premium to surplus ratios, and policy acquisition costs as a percentage of net earned premiums. But, once again, the more familiar ratios like ROE, debt-to-capital, price-to-earnings, and price-to-book ratios provide valuable information as well.

I gave you the curveball; now for the slider: the metrics stressed in this book can sometimes be misleading, even for businesses in industries that the metrics normally apply well to. I will provide you with three examples using companies that many of you are probably familiar with, whether you own shares in the businesses or not. This is not a recommendation to buy or sell any shares in Apple, DirecTV, or Costco. This analysis is simply provided as a teaching tool to demonstrate that the numbers (metrics) don't always tell the whole story.

Apple has very strong fundamentals.[79] It has $145 billion in cash. In 2012, it had a FCF margin of 27%, and over the past seven years its average FCF margin was 22%. Apple's 2012 ROE was 35% and it has averaged 27% ROE over the past seven years. Apple's valuation, at least at first glance, appears attractive as well. At the time of this writing, Apple's stock price is about $410 per share (down from $700). At $410, Apple's price-to-earnings ratio is 9x (using trailing 12-month earnings), versus Apple's five-year average P/E of 15x and the S&P 500 P/E of 18x. If you back out the $153 in cash per share, Apple is selling at only 6x earnings. Apple generated about $42 billion of free cash flow in 2012 and its price-to-free cash flow is 9.5x, less than the 10x threshold that I look for. Looking at this snapshot of Apple, it qualifies as one of my 20-20-10 businesses, those businesses with at least a 20% FCF margin and at least a 20% ROE and selling at less than 10x FCF.

No one can deny that Apple has exciting fundamentals. But what concerns me is the valuation, even at less than 10x FCF. I will now try to answer the all-important question of "why" Apple is selling at a low multiple.

The market typically awards a company a high price-to-earnings ratio if (1) the company is a high-growth company (like Netflix, Amazon.com, and Lululemon) or (2) it has stable and predictable earnings (like a consumer staples company).[80] But currently, Apple is experiencing slowing growth and shrinking profit margins, and its lack of innovation has caused the market to lose confidence and

---

[79] Disclosure: The author does not currently and has never owned shares of Apple.

[80] Housel, Morgan. "2 Types of Companies Deserve High Valuations," available at http://www.fool.com/investing/general/2013/03/25/2-types-of-companies-deserve-high-valuations.aspx?source=isesitlnk0000001&mrr=1.00 (6/29/2013).

excitement in Apple's future earnings power. On April 23, 2013, the *Financial Times* Lex Team wrote, "Their trailing p/e ratio is below 10. But until the clouds part and Apple's next innovative product appears, Apple is a large tech company with decelerating or possibly falling growth. This kind of company trades at p/e ratios of about 10 or perhaps a notch or two more. Dividends and cash piles do not make much difference (see Microsoft)."[81] Similarly, on June 29, 2012, Morgan Housel of The Motley Fool wrote, "Many have wondered recently why Apple trades at a fairly low valuation given its success. It may be because investors finally realize that companies like Apple must reinvent themselves every few years, imagining, designing, and engineering entirely new products. What are the odds one of those reinventions won't live up to past successes? Quite high. Yet the odds that consumers will still be using the same toothpaste 20 years from now are good, as are the odds that Colgate will still own a sizable share of the market."[82]

I know Apple is a strong business and a great brand. But I honestly don't know if Apple is cheap here or not, and that is precisely why I don't own it. I don't know what Apple will be selling in five or 10 years, whether it will be iPhones, iPads, iTVs, iWatches, iCars, or something else entirely, and I don't know who its competition will be. Even more, I don't know for sure that consumers will even be using cell phones and tablets a decade from now. Without more clarity, I will pass every time, accepting that I will miss a lot of multibaggers along the way. I missed huge returns in Apple once, and I would not be surprised if I miss them again. But I'm just looking

---

[81] "Apple: Far From the Tree," available at http://www.ft.com/intl/cms/s/3/f9e6b848-ac60-11e2-a063-00144feabdc0.html#axzz2Xd8ICSsz (6/29/2013). Note: only premium subscribers will have access to this article.

[82] Housel, Morgan. "Why Simple Investments Win," available at http://www.fool.com/investing/general/2012/06/29/simple-wins.aspx?source=isesitlnk0000001&mrr=0.17 (6/29/2013).

for simple ideas in which I can formulate clear and easy answers to the seven questions I posed in the chapter on research. Just to be clear, I'm not saying Apple is too expensive to buy. I'm just saying that I personally don't have enough confidence in my valuation of Apple to buy.

DirecTV is another example in which the metrics discussed in this book don't tell the whole story.[83] DirecTV is a satellite TV provider in the United States and Latin America. It has 35 million customers and generated about $2.3 billion in free cash flow in 2012. Its FCF margin is a respectable 8% ($2.3 billion in FCF divided by $29.7 billion in revenue). But DirecTV has negative shareholders' equity (also referred to as a shareholder deficit). Since DirecTV has negative shareholders' equity, it has a negative return on equity (ROE), which is the primary performance metric of a business (remember that ROE is net income divided by shareholders' equity). But, as I said, the metrics can be misleading.

DirectTV uses its free cash flow (plus a large amount of debt) to buy back tons of its own stock. When I say "tons," that is not an exaggeration. On May 14, 2013, the *Wall Street Journal* pointed out that DirecTV has repurchased 57% of its shares outstanding since the beginning of 2006, a higher percentage than any other company in the S&P 500.[84]

When a company repurchases stock at a price above its book value (but it could still be buying below intrinsic value), it has the effect of reducing book value per share. When a company repurchases stock above book value on the scale of DirecTV, it can reduce book value per share so much that it results in negative sharehold-

---

[83] Disclosure: The author does not currently and has never owned shares of DirecTV.

[84] Murphy, Maxwell. "Buybacks Boost Some Companies' Earnings," available at http://blogs. wsj.com/cfo/2013/05/14/buybacks-boost-some-companies-earnings/?KEYWORDS=DirecT V+repurchases+57+of+shares (6/29/2013).

ers' equity. If you are interested in a detailed explanation of the accounting, DirecTV explains in its 2006 10-K report how the buybacks impact its shareholders' equity.[85] But, if you look back to 2006, the year that DirecTV started its massive buyback program, you will see it had positive shareholders' equity and was generating about 20% returns on equity.

In DirecTV's case, if you think the stock is selling at a meaningful discount to its intrinsic value, then management may be doing shareholders a favor buying back all that stock because by reducing the number of shares outstanding, it is increasing an owner's percentage share of the company. In other words, shareholders in DirecTV will see their ownership increase even if they don't buy any additional shares, because DirecTV is doing the buying for them.

In addition to its massive share repurchase program, DirecTV may capture an investor's interest because of its growth opportunities in Latin America and its remarkable efficiency as measured by revenue per employee.[86] On April 9, 2012, the *Wall Street Journal* reported that S&P 500 companies had average revenue per employee of $420,000 in 2011.[87] In both 2011 and 2012, DirecTV generated more than $1 million in revenue per employee, more than double the market average. Regarding the opportunity to service the growing middle class in Latin America, the DirecTV 2011 Annual Report states, "In Latin America, we continued to benefit from the growing population of young consumers – some 70 percent of the population is under the age of 40 – entering their high earning

---

[85] DirecTV 2006 10-K, p. 96, available at http://investor.directv.com/annuals.cfm (6/29/2013).

[86] Thank you to Joe Magyer at The Motley Fool for helping me better understand the DirecTV story!!!

[87] Thurm, Scott. "For Big Companies, Life Is Good," available at http://online.wsj.com/article/SB10001424052702303815404577331660464739018.html (6/29/2013).

years and living in growing economies not heavily tied to the mature U.S. or European markets. Pay-TV is the ultimate middle-class product and we remain well positioned to meet their entertainment needs."[88]

Although I did not single out profit margins as one of the metrics stressed in this book, understanding a company's margin profile is critical to understanding the profitability of the industry and the company's position within the industry. Margins vary across industries. Some industries enjoy higher levels of profitability than other industries, and some companies enjoy higher margins than their competitors within the same industry. In general, the higher the profit margins, the better. Costco turns this theory on its head.[89]

Costco is a membership warehouse club with stores in the United States, Puerto Rico, Canada, Mexico, Asia, and Australia. Whereas most companies try to maximize profits, Costco tries to shrink its profit margins to the lowest level possible. Its strategy is to offer its members (who pay entry level fees of only $55 per year) the lowest possible prices by selling products as close to cost as is feasible. Costco's 2012 annual report celebrates its margin contraction: "Our gross margin (net sales less merchandise costs) as a percent of net sales decreased in fiscal 2012, largely due to our investment in lowering prices, which is consistent with our goal of maintaining price and value leadership. This is what we do...each and every day!"[90]

Costco's laser-like focus on providing its members with the best value and service leads to huge brand loyalty. Costco has over 60

---

[88] DirecTV 2011 Annual Report, p. 20, available at http://investor.directv.com/annuals.cfm (6/29/2013).

[89] Disclosure: The author does not currently and has never owned shares of Costco.

[90] Costco 2012 Annual Report, p. 2, available at http://phx.corporate-ir.net/phoenix.zhtml?c=83830&p=irol-reportsannual (6/29/2013).

million members (including both primary cardholders and additional cardholders) and enjoys membership renewal rates of 90% in the U.S. and 86% globally. Costco's membership fees contribute only 2% of sales but 75% of operating income, which gives you an idea of just how thin its gross margins are (or just how close to cost Costco sells its products).[91]

In its 2012 annual report Costco clearly explains its strategy and its ability to generate strong cash flows despite low gross margins. Costco sells bulk sizes of a limited number of brand-name and private-label products across a broad range of product categories. It sells these products cheaply, which leads to high sales volume and inventory turnover. The 2012 report states, "This turnover, when combined with the operating efficiencies achieved by volume purchasing, efficient distribution and reduced handling of merchandise in no-frills, self-service warehouse facilities, enables us to operate profitably at significantly lower gross margins than traditional wholesalers, mass merchandisers, supermarkets, and supercenters." The report continues, "Because of our high sales volume and rapid inventory turnover, we generally sell inventory before we are required to pay many of our merchandise vendors, even though we take advantage of early payment discounts when available. To the extent that sales increase and inventory turnover becomes more rapid, a greater percentage of inventory is financed through payment terms provided by suppliers rather than by working capital."[92] This rapid inventory turnover and limited need for working capital leads to respectable returns (remember that asset turns are a driver of ROE) and free cash flow (less working capital

---

[91] Ibid., p. 29.

[92] Ibid., pp. 8-9.

means more free cash), which is used to open new stores, pay an increasing dividend, and buy back stock.

Costco's purchasing strategy deserves special attention. In a July 17, 2005, article titled "How Costco Became the Anti-Wal-Mart" in the *New York Times*, Steven Greenhouse explains, "A typical Costco store stocks 4,000 types of items, including perhaps just four toothpaste brands, while a Wal-Mart typically stocks more than 100,000 types of items and may carry 60 sizes and brands of toothpastes. Narrowing the number of options increases the sales volume of each, allowing Costco to squeeze deeper and deeper bulk discounts from suppliers."[93] As the *Times* article shows, Costco is absolutely fanatical about demanding the lowest possible prices from its suppliers. This unrelenting pursuit on cutting its merchandise costs is the driving force behind the value proposition Costco can offer its members, a proposition that engenders intense member loyalty. This member loyalty, in turn, leads to increased sales, which lead to even greater leverage over suppliers, which leads to even lower prices and increased sales volume, supporting a virtuous circle. Even though online competition is a significant challenge for Costco going forward, a June 6, 2013, article on Bloomberg Businessweek.com said that at the present time not even Amazon has lower prices than Costco.[94]

The Greenhouse article in the *New York Times* mentioned above is primarily a profile of Jim Sinegal, Costco's founder and now former CEO. Jim Sinegal is the type of manager I want to invest with. The article quotes Mr. Sinegal as saying, "On Wall Street, they're in

---

[93] Greenhouse, Steven. "How Costco Became the Anti-Wal-Mart," available at http://www.nytimes.com/2005/07/17/business/yourmoney/17costco.html?_r=0 (6/29/2013).

[94] Stone, Brad. "Costco CEO Craig Jelinek Leads the Cheapest, Happiest Company in the World," available at http://www.businessweek.com/articles/2013-06-06/costco-ceo-craig-jelinek-leads-the-cheapest-happiest-company-in-the-world (6/29/2013).

the business of making money between now and next Thursday. I don't say that with any bitterness, but we can't take that view. We want to build a company that will still be here 50 and 60 years from now."[95] As a long-term investor, that should be music to your ears. Here is some more music. The article says that Jim Sinegal's base salary was only $350,000 for the year (plus a $200,000 bonus).[96] This below-average industry pay applies to Costco's current CEO, Craig Jelinek, as well. Costco pays its front-line employees well above average industry wages and pays its executive management fairly but well below average industry compensation levels. Look it up. You might be impressed.

Costco's competitive advantages (remarkable purchasing power by focusing on a limited number of SKUs, intensely loyal members, and a corporate culture that recognizes the importance of keeping things simple, keeping members happy, and treating shareholders as owners) are plainly obvious, and I believe Costco to be an example of a finely run business.

So, here we have three companies: one where 10x FCF may not be a bargain price (Apple), one that may be a good investment despite negative returns on equity (DirecTV), and one that has a huge competitive advantage despite razor-thin profit margins (Costco). The lesson here is that investors should not blindly make buy and sell decisions based on the "numbers" alone. Simply looking at a spreadsheet of numbers rarely tells you the complete story. You must dig deeper to uncover what is behind the numbers. I think far too many investors spend far too much time on their models and not nearly enough time just thinking about industry trends, whether the business has a competitive advantage, the durability

---

[95] Greenhouse, Steven. "How Costco Became the Anti-Wal-Mart," available at http://www.nytimes.com/2005/07/17/business/yourmoney/17costco.html?_r=0 (6/29/2013).

[96] Ibid.

of that advantage, and what can go wrong. To reiterate, you must understand the industry and where the business fits within the industry. I firmly believe that qualitative analysis is just as important as quantitative analysis, if not more so. I personally stopped building complex models about two years ago so that I can spend more time reading and thinking.

In the above analysis of Apple, DirecTV, and Costco I cited information from the *Financial Times*, the *Wall Street Journal*, the *New York Times*, and Bloomberg Businessweek.com. I want to stress again that investors can get valuable information by reading newspapers and news magazines. Newspapers and company filings are my two primary sources of information, and I probably spend equal time between the two sources. In addition to the *Wall Street Journal*, the *Financial Times*, and the *New York Times*, I read *Bloomberg Businessweek* and *Fortune* magazine on a pretty regular basis, among others.

I reference newspapers, news magazines, and company reports to demonstrate the vast amount of knowledge available to investors at a very reasonable cost (company filings are free and newspapers and magazines are well worth the price). All you have to do is read them. As I mentioned earlier, if you don't have the time or desire to read quality journalism and company reports, and the ability to interpret the information and make quality investments, then it's probably best to put your money in an index fund.

CONCLUSION

Take a simple idea and take it seriously. (Charlie Munger, Poor Charlie's Almanack, *Expanded Third Edition, p. 53)*

Over the past five years, my good friend and mentor Charles Mizrahi has reminded me that "when you buy good businesses at good prices, good things tend to happen." He is right. Both his *Hidden Values Alert* newsletter and *Inevitable Wealth Portfolio* newsletter are top-rated newsletters according to the *Hulbert Financial Digest*. The stocks he has recommended have absolutely trounced the market.[97] I have also been very pleased with my own results. Since February of 2009, I have generated 21% annualized returns versus the S&P 500, which has returned 18.5% over the same time frame. I beat the market on the way up, and since I own a concentrated portfolio of a few compounding machines (that I will probably own forever) and a few solid businesses that I still consider decently undervalued, I am confident I can beat the market on the way down. If I can keep up with the market on the way up, and minimize losses on the way down, I'll end up with a very acceptable long-term result. That should be your objective as well.

But my 20% returns need to be put into perspective. I started managing real money near the market lows of the Great Recession (part luck and part strategy) and the market has since reached new highs. This had been a magical ride for the stock market and for my

---

[97]Newslettersareavailableatwww.hiddenvaluesalert.comandhttp://inevitablewealthportfolio.com/.

portfolio and I guarantee you I will not be able to maintain 20% annual returns going forward. Businesses are just not as cheap today as they were back then. But if I stick to the principles that I have laid out in this book, I'll do just fine. And probably better than fine.

I believe some parts of investing are simpler than others. Finding a company that you understand and admire, evaluating its fundamentals, and determining with a certain level of confidence if a company is over- or undervalued is the simpler part. Yet people make it more difficult and esoteric than it needs to be. At the very least you can determine if a company is too hard to understand (falls outside of your circle of competence) and move on. But the art of investing (which requires patience, emotional discipline, and the courage to resist the crowd) is terribly difficult to master. If you don't have the emotional makeup necessary to succeed as an individual stock picker, then you should just invest in an index fund, close your eyes, and turn off the TV. Do not listen to all the doom-and-gloom you hear on TV and do not fret about daily movements in the market. I guarantee the market (and your portfolio, which is designed to mimic the market if you are in an index fund) will have down years. I guarantee you will have years when you lose money on paper. But I am also confident that over time the markets will continue to reach new highs and that those people who remain substantially invested for the remainder of their lives will end up comfortably rich. There is absolutely no shame in indexing!

But if you do decide you are ready to manage your own portfolio, my advice to you is to stick to investing in businesses that have a simple investing thesis (i.e., the company has been profitable and generated high returns for years and is likely to continue to do so; it commands a large market share; and it has intense brand loyalty, is run by good managers, and is selling at an attractive price). But if management needs to pull off a heroic turnaround and the stars have to align to realize your required return, before investing always remember there are other opportunities for your capital.

From both study and practice, I learned that investing is about understanding the drivers of business value and how to calculate that value. Investing is about understanding market dynamics and business dynamics. Investing is about choosing the best alternative for your capital. Investing is about minimizing permanent loss by strictly buying at a discount to intrinsic value to allow for a margin of safety. Investing is about vigilance and hard work and investing a meaningful amount when you find a no-brainer. Investing is about learning from our mistakes and the mistakes of others and embracing the learning process. Perhaps most important of all, successful investing is about having the emotional discipline to hold on for the ride and understanding that a few basic principles (in this case 17 of them) can go a long way. Best of luck, and remember 10x FCF (or less)!!!

APPENDIX 1: UNDERSTANDING STOCK RETURNS, THE P/E RATIO, AND OTHER VALUATION MULTIPLES

First, what is the stock market and what is a stock? The stock market is a place (although today most transactions are done electronically over the Internet) where millions of people get together to buy and sell shares of businesses (stocks). The stock market is just like any other market. Picture a flea market. At a flea market, people come together to buy and sell stuff. Some of the goods are fine merchandise and some of the goods are of lesser quality. The stock market is the same. Some of the businesses for sale are high-quality, and others are struggling for survival.[98] Unlike a flea market, however, where individuals buy something they are uniquely interested in, participants in the stock market feel pressured to buy what everyone else is buying and to sell what everyone else is selling. Don't do this!!! The stock market is often wrong in its valuation of businesses, and as a market participant you are never forced to buy or sell anything. Rather than follow the crowd, block out the noise and rely on your own research of individual businesses. I hope this concept of ignoring what the market is doing will become clearer throughout the book.

---

[98] This book advocates buying quality businesses, but investing in distressed companies can also be very profitable because distressed companies can be purchased at very cheap prices.

When you buy a stock you are purchasing ownership in the company. When you buy a bond you are providing a loan to that company (or in the case of Treasuries, you are lending money to the government). So, if you own stock in Apple, you are an owner of Apple (one of many owners, but an owner nonetheless) and are entitled to a percentage of the company's earnings (net income). Those earnings may be paid out as dividends or retained for future growth. If you buy an Apple bond, you have loaned money to Apple and will receive interest payments in return.[99] This book will focus on stocks.

Price-to-Earnings Ratio

Most stocks trade based on a multiple of earnings. This multiple is called the price-to-earnings ratio (P/E ratio). Stocks trade on earnings because when you buy a stock you are buying a percentage of the company's future earnings (or profits).

A P/E of 15x means you are paying $15 for every $1 of earnings per share. The P/E represents how long in years it would take you to make back your original investment (or break even on your investment) if earnings remained constant. In other words, if the company continues to earn $1 per share annually, it would take you 15 years to break even. Obviously, we want to break even sooner rather than later, so a lower P/E indicates a cheaper stock.

But looking at the P/E ratio in isolation (not comparing it to anything) will tell you virtually nothing. In general, you should

---

[99] Bonds are called fixed-income securities because the investor receives a fixed amount (the same amount) of cash on a regular basis until the bond matures. Once the bond matures, the investor receives the face value of the bond and nothing more. Bond holders get paid before shareholders in the event of a bankruptcy. Shareholders are owners, meaning they are entitled to a percentage of the profits and gain voting rights and possibly a dividend. Earnings and dividends are not fixed: The earnings per share can increase, the dividend can increase, and the stock price can rise in value. Earnings per share can also decrease, the company can cut or eliminate its dividend, and the stock price can go to zero.

look to buy solid companies (see Chapter 2, What to Buy) trading at a discount to (1) their historical average P/E, (2) the industry (or peer) average P/E, and/or (3) the market P/E (the S&P 500 has historically traded at about 15x-16x). It is important to note that a P/E ratio does not indicate a company's intrinsic value. It simply tells you if the business is underpriced or overpriced <u>relative</u> to its own history or relative to a group.

Stock Returns

Stocks provide returns in three ways: (1) earnings growth, (2) price-to-earnings multiple expansion, and/or (3) dividends. A simple example will illustrate:

If a company generates $1 in earnings per share (EPS) and its stock price is $10, then the P/E ratio is 10 (stock price of $10 divided by EPS of $1 is 10). Theoretically, the first way stock prices move higher is if earnings grow. So assume that in the following year earnings grow to $2 per share and the stock price appreciates to $20. In this case, the stock goes up based on earnings growth, even though the multiple stays constant at 10x (stock price of $20 divided by EPS of $2 is 10).

The second way stocks appreciate is if earnings remain constant but the market is willing to award those earnings a higher multiple. For example, assume now that EPS is the original $1, but the stock price goes up to $20 per share. In this case, the earnings remained the same, but the P/E multiple increased to 20x (stock price of $20 divided by EPS of $1 is 20). Obviously, the best case for returns would be if both earnings increase and the multiple expands. If earnings increase to $2 per share and the market is willing to place a 20x multiple on those earnings, now the investor has a $40 stock (stock price of $40 divided by EPS of $2 is a P/E of 20).

Finally, stocks that pay dividends can generate additional returns from the dividend yield.

It is crucial to understand that if you buy stock in a company whose earnings power is sure to be higher years down the road, it does not automatically mean the stock will sell at a higher price years down the road. If the stock was originally purchased at a very high multiple of earnings (high P/E ratio), the stock price may linger as earnings climb upward but the multiple falls back down to earth. In other words, the higher earnings and lower multiple could essentially cancel each other out and the stock could fail to appreciate, or at least fail to appreciate by an amount commensurate with the earnings growth. Companies whose stocks trade at unsustainably high multiples of earnings often come crashing down when Wall Street realizes that the high growth rates cannot possibly go on forever.

PEG Ratio

It is also useful to compare the stock's P/E ratio to its growth rate in earnings. This method is often called the PE-to-growth, or PEG, ratio. The PEG ratio says that a stock is fairly valued if its P/E ratio is equal to its expected growth rate in earnings (a PEG of 1) and that it is preferable to buy stocks trading at a discount to earnings growth. In other words, the lower the PEG, the cheaper the stock. Assume two companies that are in the same industry: one is projected to grow earnings at an annualized rate of 20% in the next five years and has a P/E ratio of 20 (so PEG ratio is 20/20 = 1) and the other is also projected to grow earnings at 20% but has a P/E ratio of 12 (so PEG ratio is 12/20 = 0.6). On the surface, it appears that the second company is cheaper, but as an investor you would also need to research why the second company is trading at such a discounted P/E multiple. Always ask why something is cheap!!!

Additionally, you should never buy a stock on P/E ratio alone. For example, suppose one company in the cassette tape industry has a P/E ratio of 8x and another company in the energy industry has a P/E ratio of 15x. The cassette tape company appears cheaper on strictly a P/E basis, but the company is operating in a shrinking (no-growth) industry, whereas the energy company may have attractive growth potential ahead of it. In the end, the company trading at 8x may prove to be far more expensive than the company trading at 15x earnings. This shows that investment analysis requires so much more than simply comparing P/E ratios.

Earnings Yield

Earnings yield is the inverse of the P/E ratio, so it is calculated as EPS divided by the stock price. Therefore, stocks with a relatively low P/E ratio will have a relatively high earnings yield. The earnings yield is a good measure of expected (or forward rate of) return because it represents how much investors receive in earnings relative to how much they pay. Value investors want to buy earnings cheaply. Since value investors want to buy more for less, they prefer a higher earnings yield. Thinking in terms of earnings yield (as opposed to P/E ratios) allows an investor to compare the annual expected return of a stock to the risk-free rate (the yield on the 10-year Treasury bond), to a corporate bond, to other stocks, and to the yield on a real estate investment, something referred to as the cap rate (net annual cash flow divided by the purchase price of the property).

Factors Affecting the P/E Ratio (in general)[100]

<u>Earnings growth</u>: in general investors are willing to "pay up" for growth, so high-growth stocks have higher P/E ratios than low-growth stocks.

<u>Leverage</u>: in general the higher the leverage, the lower the P/E because investors won't pay up for the added risk that comes with high debt levels.

<u>Earnings visibility/predictability</u>: in general the greater the predictability and stability of earnings, the higher the P/E.

<u>Earnings volatility</u>: in general the greater the volatility (cyclicality) of earnings, the lower the P/E.

<u>Interest rates</u>: in general when interest rates go up, investors will sell stocks and move into bonds. Selling stocks drives down P/E ratios, so when interest rates are high, P/E ratios move lower.

<u>Market multiple</u>: in general, a rising tide lifts all boats, so the higher the market P/E, the higher the P/E ratio of individual stocks in the market.

Price-to-Book Ratio

Another very useful method is to value a business based upon a multiple of its net worth (or book value). The price-to-book ratio (P/B) is calculated as the stock price divided by the book value per share.

---

[100] I adapted this chart from a similar chart given to me by Professor Peter Ricchiuti. Professor Ricchiuti is an associate dean at the Tulane Freeman School of Business and the director of the Burkenroad Reports Program, one of the top equity research programs in the country. Professor Ricchiuti is a mentor and friend of mine. He is genuinely kind and outrageously funny. He gives presentations on investing and economics around the country. Check out his website at http://peterricchiuti.com/ (9/4/2013). Visit Burkenroad Reports at www.burkenroad.org/ (10/4/2013).

A company's net worth is calculated as total assets (what it owns) less total liabilities (what it owes). Whatever is left over is the company's net worth, also referred to as shareholders' equity. Businesses that can consistently earn high returns on their shareholders' equity (this return on equity metric is the primary performance metric of the firm), are often the businesses whose stocks perform best in the market over time. Because businesses that consistently earn a high return on book value are higher-quality than those that consistently earn low returns on book value, businesses with high returns on book value are worth more (more valuable) than those that earn low returns on book value. In an appendix to his 1983 letter to shareholders, Warren Buffett explains that companies that consistently earn above-average returns on tangible equity are worth more than tangible book value (perhaps they are worth 2x or 3x or even 5x tangible book value). This concept that investors should be willing to pay more than 1 times book value for a high-quality business is terribly important, and I encourage you to read Buffett's 1983 letter as soon as you can!!! Of course, if you find a high-quality business selling at an unreasonably low multiple of book value or at a discount to book value, you may have found yourself a home run.

Although useful in valuing any business, some stocks (example: financial services companies such as banks and insurance companies) trade primarily on a multiple of tangible book value. Tangible book value (TBV) is calculated as book value less goodwill and intangibles. Some analysts believe that tangible book value has a stronger meaning with banks than, say, a manufacturing firm because the vast majority of a manufacturing company's capital is allocated to property, plant, and equipment (tangible assets), but banks invest the vast majority of their capital in intangible assets (things like human capital, client relationships, and brand name).

If a bank is selling at a discount to tangible book value, it means the market is valuing the bank's intangible assets (its people, relationships, and brand name) at less than zero. Banking is based on relationships, so these "intangibles" are often sources of significant value for banks.

Price-to-Free Cash Flow Ratio

Free cash flow (FCF) is the amount of cash that a company generates after spending on capital expenditures to maintain and grow its assets. A rough measure of FCF can be calculated by subtracting capital expenditures from operating cash flow.[101] Both cash flow from operations and capital expenditures (funds spent on property, plant, and equipment) line items can be found on the company's cash flow statement. FCF can be used to grow the business (example: open new store locations), pay down debt, acquire other companies, buy back stock, or pay dividends. Any leftover cash can be used to increase the cash on the balance sheet.

Since FCF is the actual amount of cash available to owners, some investors prefer to focus on cash flow and use the price-to-free cash flow multiple for relative valuation. P/FCF is calculated as stock price divided by free cash flow per share. Free cash flow per share is simply FCF divided by the number of shares outstanding. Since investors prefer to buy FCF on the cheap, a lower P/FCF ratio is generally better.

Free Cash Flow Yield

FCF yield is the inverse of the P/FCF multiple, so it is calculated as FCF per share divided by the stock price. Similar to the earnings yield, the FCF yield is a good estimate of forward rate of return.

---

[101] To read more about FCF, please visit http://www.investopedia.com/terms/f/freecashflow. asp (9/10/2013) and http://wiki.fool.com/Free_cash_flow (9/10/2013).

Stocks with low P/FCF multiples have high FCF yields. Therefore, all else being equal, value investors prefer stocks with low P/FCF multiples and high FCF yields. Once again, thinking in terms of yield allows investors to compare expected returns from stocks to those of fixed income investments (bonds) and real estate.

Calculations

Sales = revenues (sales are for product sales and revenues are for service sales and both are referred to as the top line)

Earnings = net income (both are referred to as the bottom line)

Earnings per share (EPS) = total annual earnings/number of shares outstanding

P/E ratio = stock price/earnings per share

Earnings yield = earnings per share/stock price

PEG ratio = PE ratio/expected compound annual growth rate in earnings over the next five years

Shareholders' equity (book value) = total assets – total liabilities

Book value per share = book value/number of shares outstanding

P/B ratio = stock price/book value per share

Tangible book value = book value – goodwill and intangibles

Tangible book value per share = tangible book value/number of shares outstanding

P/TBV = stock price/tangible book value per share

Free cash flow = cash flow from operations – capital expenditures

FCF per share = free cash flow/number of shares outstanding

P/FCF = stock price/FCF per share

FCF yield = FCF per share/stock price

APPENDIX 2: CALCULATIONS

In this section, we look at two companies, one with debt and one without, but both in solid financial shape as of the writing of this book. I provide select financial data from each company's 2012 10-K filing and then demonstrate how to calculate the metrics stressed in this book. This appendix is not meant to be a comprehensive lecture on financial statement analysis but is rather a guide to calculating the few metrics discussed in this book. Understanding how to calculate the numbers is crucial, as is understanding what the numbers mean. But you can also get 10 years of company data at no charge on sites like Morningstar and GuruFocus, allowing you to track how the fundamentals are trending over a decade, without performing all the calculations by hand or punching them into a calculator or spreadsheet.

The first company is the TJX Companies (TJX), the owner and operator of T.J. Maxx, Marshalls, HomeGoods, and other retail concepts. TJX competitors include Wal-Mart, Target, Kohl's, J.C. Penney, Bed Bath & Beyond, and countless other retail brands, as well as department and outlet stores. The second company is FactSet Research Systems (FDS), a financial technology and services company that provides financial information and analytics to the finance community around the world. FactSet competitors include Bloomberg, Thomson Reuters, Standard & Poor's Capital IQ, Dow Jones, and others. Basically, FactSet provides all the metrics discussed in this book, in addition to credit analysis, portfolio analysis, modeling tools, and more.

The TJX annual reports and 10-Ks can be found at www.tjx.com and the FDS annual reports and 10-Ks can be found at www.factset.com.[102]

This is not a recommendation to buy or sell the TJX Companies or FactSet Research Systems. I am simply using each company's financials to demonstrate how to calculate the metrics focused on in this book.

TJX Companies financial data taken from 2012 10-K, pp. F3-F6:

Sales: $25,878,372

Income before provision for income taxes: 3,077,351

Provision for income taxes: 1,170,664

Interest expense: 29,175

***By adding income before provision for income taxes and the interest expense, you will get the earnings before interest and taxes (EBIT), which is also called operating income. So, EBIT is equal to 3,077,351 + 29,175, which is 3,106,526.

***By dividing provision for income taxes by the income before provision you get the tax rate. So, the tax rate is 1,170,664/3,077,351, which is 38%.

Net income: 1,906,687

Average shares outstanding: 747,555

Cash and cash equivalents: 1,811,957

Long-term debt: 774,552

Shareholders' equity: 3,665,937

Net cash provided by operating activities (cash flow from operations): 3,045,614

Property additions (capital expenditures): 978,228

---

[102] Disclosure: The author owns shares of both TJX Companies and FactSet Research Systems.

TJX Calculations:

Net cash = cash and cash equivalents minus long-term debt

Net cash = 1,811,957 − 774,552 = 1,037,405 (a little more than $1 billion in net cash)

Debt/equity = debt/shareholders' equity (in this case TJX has only long-term debt, so long-term debt is equal to total debt)

Debt/equity = 774,552/3,665,937 = 21%

LTD/total capital = LTD/(LTD + shareholders' equity)

LTD/total capital = 774,552/(774,552 + 3,665,937) = 17%

Return on equity = net income/shareholders' equity

Return on equity = 1,906,687/3,665,937 = 52%

Return on invested capital = (EBIT*(1-tax rate))/(LTD + shareholders' equity)

Return on invested capital = (3,106,526*(1 - 0.38))/(774,552 + 3,665,937) = 43%

Free cash flow = operating cash flow minus capital expenditures

Free cash flow = 3,045,614 − 978,228 = 2,067,386 (that's a little over $2 billion in FCF generation)

Free cash flow margin = FCF/sales

Free cash flow margin = 2,067,386/25,878,372 = 8%

Free cash flow per share = FCF/the number of shares outstanding

Free cash flow per share = 2,067,386/747,555 = 2.77

Price/FCF = current stock price/FCF per share (the stock price at the time of this writing is $50 per share)

Price/FCF = 50/2.77 = 18x

FCF yield = FCF per share/stock price

FCF yield = 2.77/50 = 5.5%

$EBIT = income \ before \ provision \ for \ income \ tax + interest \ expense$

***One metric I mentioned in the book but did not discuss in detail is the **interest coverage ratio**, which is calculated as **EBIT/interest expense**. This ratio measures how many times a company's operating income (EBIT) can cover its annual interest expense (i.e., how easily the company can service its debt) and is an important measure of a company's financial health. TJX's interest coverage ratio is 3,106,526/29,175, which is 107x, an unbelievably safe number, since I like to see a ratio of at least 5x. To be fair, I used $29,175 for interest expense, which is net of $7,750 in capitalized interest and net of $11,657 in interest income. But even if I use the total interest expense of $48,582, TJX still has an interest coverage ratio of 3,106,526/48,582, which is still a stellar 64x.

FactSet Research Systems financial data taken from 2012 10-K, pp. 52-54:

Revenues: $805,793

Operating income (EBIT): 272,990

Income before income taxes: 274,705 (this is 272,990 in operating income plus 1,715 in "other income")

Provision for income taxes: 85,896

Net income: 188,809

Average shares outstanding: 45,810

Cash and cash equivalents: 189,044

Long-term debt: 0

Stockholders' equity: 552,264

Net cash provided by operating activities: 231,965

Purchase of property, equipment, and leasehold improvements (capital expenditures): 22,520

FDS Calculations:

Net cash = 189,044 – 0 = 189,044 (a little over $189 million in net cash)

Debt/equity = 0/552,264 = 0 (FDS has zero short- or long-term debt)

LTD/total capital = 0/(0 + 552,264) = 0

Return on equity = 188,809/552,264 = 34%

Tax rate = 85,896/274,705 = 31% (or .31 written as a decimal)

Return on invested capital = (272,990*(1 - 0.31))/(0 + 552,264) = 34%

Free cash flow = 231,965 – 22,520 = 209,445

Free cash flow margin = 209,445/805,793 = 26%

Free cash flow per share = 209,445/45,810 = 4.57

Price/FCF = 100/4.57 = 22x (the stock price at the time of this writing is $100 per share)

FCF yield = 4.57/100 = 4.57%

APPENDIX 3: THE ANNUAL REPORT

In the previous appendix, we see that TJX and FactSet Research Systems are both financially strong companies that generated a lot of cash and earned high returns in 2012. By looking back five or 10 years, you will see that 2012 was not an anomaly for either company. Both TJX and FactSet have a history of consistently increasing revenues (the top line) and earnings (the bottom line) and generating above-average returns. It is helpful to study not only a company's most recent filings, but to go back at least five years to see how things are trending at the company and to see if management is achieving (and sticking to) the goals that it set for the company in previous years. In this section, I create bullet points from TJX and FactSet's annual reports, going back at least five years, to show what captured my attention and to help paint a picture of each company's business model, growth, and competitive position. Once again, you can find TJX reports at www.tjx.com and FactSet reports at www.factset.com.

The following should not be used as a recommendation to buy or sell shares of the TJX Companies or FactSet Research Systems. I am simply trying to demonstrate the type of information that can be gathered by reading company filings. My goal with Appendix 3 is to show that simply calculating the numbers in Appendix 2 is not enough; investors should also read company reports and filings (and other sources) in order to understand how the numbers are generated and what the numbers mean. After reading my bullet points, it will be no secret that I think, at present time, the TJX Companies and FactSet are quality businesses. But this is in no way a recommendation to buy (or sell) TJX or FactSet. For one, the price you pay is a critical component of investment success and I have not provided my thoughts on their valuations. Additionally, market fundamentals and company fundamentals are dynamic. The fundamentals could be drastically different when you read this book than they were when I wrote the book. These appendixes are meant for instructional purposes only!

The TJX Companies:
- TJX's pricing strategy is to offer brand-name goods at 20% to 60% less than the competition. (TJX 2006 Annual Report, p. 1)
- The shopping experience at TJX stores has the feel of a treasure hunt. Since TJX ships new merchandise to the stores almost daily, shoppers visit the stores more often and buy more often because they know an item they like will most likely not be in the store on their next visit. (TJX 2006 Annual Report, p. 3)
- TJX generates some of the highest returns on equity and returns on invested capital in the retail industry. (TJX 2007 Annual Report, pp. 9-10)
- TJX's inventories turn nine times per year (remember that inventory turns are a driver of ROE) and it has increased same store sales (sales from stores open at least a year) in 32 out of the past 33 years. Also, TJX is one of the only U.S. retailers to have success in Europe, and it thinks Europe will continue to provide strong growth opportunities going forward. (TJX 2009 Annual Report, p. 3)

- TJX is taking significant market share from the competition. (TJX 2010 Annual Report, p. 3)
- TJX is able to order merchandise with much shorter lead times than the competition, meaning its offering is always fresh and on trend. (TJX 2010 Annual Report, p. 5)
- Short ordering times allow TJX to have one of the most flexible business models in all of retail. This allows it to quickly adjust merchandise based on current fashion trends and to adjust prices based on economic trends, all the while staying comfortably profitable. (TJX 2010 Annual Report, pp. 5-6)
- TJX isn't affected by rapidly changing fashion trends like other retailers are. Its team of 800 buyers sources merchandise from over 16,000 vendors around the world, allowing TJX to feature whichever products and brands are hot at the time. (TJX 2012 Annual Report, p. 5)
- TJX is the only major off-price retailer in Europe and it sees a long runway of growth potential there. (TJX 2012 Annual Report, p. 6)
- TJX is buying back a lot of stock and has increased the dividend for 17 straight years. Over those 17 years, the dividend has grown at a compound annual rate of 23%. (TJX 2012 Annual Report, p. 9)
- TJX generated about $26 billion in sales in 2012. It has a goal to reach $40 billion plus in sales. It plans to do so by building new stores both domestically and abroad, continuing to win market share from the competition (to get more people to shop at its existing stores), and expanding its e-commerce initiative. (TJX 2012 Annual Report, p. 1)

When researching a company, I spend a lot of time contemplating what can go wrong (i.e., what are the risk factors?). Like so many

other successful brick-and-mortar operations, in my opinion, one of TJX's biggest challenges going forward will be fending off online competition and developing its own online presence that complements its retail locations, resonates with customers, and is profitable.

- TJX is still in the early stages of developing an online offering and plans to launch a T.J. Maxx website in the second half of 2013. (TJX 2012 Annual Report, p. 7)

FactSet Research:

- FactSet's free cash flow is often higher than net income, indicating the high quality of its earnings. (FDS 2007 Annual Report, p. 5)[103]
- FactSet's client retention rate is about 95%. (FDS 2007 Annual Report, p. 5)
- FactSet grew during the Great Recession, when most other companies were struggling. (FDS 2008 Annual Report, p. 2)
- FactSet also grew in 2009 and is taking market share from the competition. (FDS 2009 Annual Report, p. 6)
- FactSet was named to *Fortune* magazine's prestigious list of the "100 Best Companies to Work For," which is a sign of a healthy company culture. (FDS 2010 Annual Report, p. 3)
- Free cash flow was once again higher than net income in 2010. (FDS 2010 Annual Report, p. 3)
- FactSet's vast offering of proprietary databases provides it with a competitive advantage and strong growth potential. (FDS 2011 Annual Report, p. 2)

---

[103] Net income is an accounting number used for reporting purposes. Free cash flow is the actual amount of cash available to owners. Reported earnings (net income) can be manipulated (both lawfully and unlawfully) easier than it is to manipulate the cash flows entering and leaving the business.

- FactSet's market share increased further. (FDS 2011 Annual Report, p. 4)
- FactSet is one of only three U.S. companies to increase revenues and earnings every year since 1996. (FDS 2012 Annual Report, p. 2)
- FactSet has increased its dividend by at least 10% for seven straight years. (FDS 2012 Annual Report, p. 5)
- FactSet's proprietary content provides it with a competitive advantage. Its unique offering is hard to replicate, and many financial firms have become so reliant on FactSet's technology for day-to-day activities that clients may face high switching costs (example: the cost to train employees in a new system or the cost of employees unhappy with software that is either inferior or that they are less familiar with, etc.) should they choose to switch to another platform. (FDS 2012 10-K, p. 9)

But FactSet is facing online competition as well.
- Recently, the availability of competing, but less complete, sets of data and content than is offered by FactSet is being offered for free (or for relatively modest costs) over the Internet. This competition could potentially impact FactSet's profits, cash flows, and growth going forward. (FDS 2012 10-K, p. 16)

APPENDIX 4: MAINTAINING A WATCH LIST

What do you do when you find a company you want to own but determine that it is too expensive to buy at the current price? Do you roll the dice and buy anyway? Of course not. Do you just forget about the name, erase it from your memory, and move on? Of course not. Rather you should put the stock on your watch list. A watch list is a list of companies that you don't currently own but that you have researched and continue to monitor so that you will be ready to buy if the stock falls to an attractive price. Remember that research should be done prior to buying, not after, and this is what maintaining a watch list allows you to do.

If a company is on my watch list, at a minimum I have read the most recent annual report and 10-K filing (but most likely I have been following the company for years and have read years of reports), the Value Line report, and any reports written by The Motley Fool. I also keep track of all my stocks by using The Motley Fool's watch list tool.

Below I demonstrate the minimum I think you should know about a company on your watch list in order to be prepared to buy. You should understand the business and the industry it operates in. You should know who the competitors are and where the growth opportunities will come from. You should be aware of who has the leading market share in the industry and which competitors are gaining share (winning new business) and which are losing share (losing business). And you should spend a lot of time thinking about the risks and what could go wrong. You should have reviewed the financials and thought about the valuation. The following is for educational purposes only and should not be used as a reason to buy or sell Rollins Inc.[104]

Rollins Inc. is the parent company of Orkin Pest Control, and the largest pest control company in the world. Bugs are not going away, and in fact they seem to be getting worse (mosquitos are carrying deadly diseases, and many cities are struggling with bedbug outbreaks). The service is absolutely essential, even in a weak economy, and the business model can't be displaced by the Internet. Until the Internet can learn to virtually beam insect fighting chemicals and other devices through the cloud, Rollins's business is relatively safe. Rollins services not just homes, but businesses too. We all agree we don't want pests where we lay our head, and having a bug or rodent problem at a restaurant or healthcare facility is not only a health hazard, but also hazardous to a business's health. Just ask a business owner how fast his restaurant would take a hit if a rodent scurries across the dining room floor or a roach is found in the food, or ask a retailer how quickly it would lose customers if bedbugs or ants are living in the clothing and feeding on shoppers. Sound gross? That's precisely why businesses pay for the service, even in tough economic environments. I can think of few services more important to health and peace of mind than pest control. Pest control is a beautiful business, and as the industry leader, Rollins has experienced 15 straight years of increased revenues and earn-

---

[104] Disclosure: The author does not currently and has never owned shares of Rollins. Also, I am not commenting on Rollins's valuation. I am just using my analysis of Rollins to demonstrate the minimum level of research needed for a company to be on your watch list. This is not a recommendation to buy or sell Rollins.

ings. (Note: I have intentionally not included the metrics, to encourage you to perform those calculations on your own.)

Where will the growth come from? First, it will come from an improving economy. As the economy grows, new homes will be built, new households will be formed, and new businesses will be created. These new homes and businesses will require pest control. If the economy temporarily falters, no worries. Rollins still has its recurring revenue stream from existing service contracts. Additional growth will come from acquisitions. Rollins has only one major competitor (Terminix) in the U.S., and the rest of the industry is controlled by a handful of mom-and-pop shops. Rollins will buy market share (buy new customer contracts) and expand geographically by strategically acquiring mom-and-pop pest control businesses. Rollins generally does not need to use debt to fund these acquisitions (it uses its cash flows), and it is often the buyer of choice, because Rollins is the parent to some of the most respected pest control brands in the industry. In other words, mom-and-pop businesses looking to sell look to Rollins first because they want to become part of the Rollins family. Rollins's many subsidiaries maintain their own name and identity, but they share their knowledge and expertise, thereby strengthening the operations of the subsidiaries and of the company as a whole.

Although Rollins has an attractive business model and decent growth opportunities, we always have to ask what can go wrong. In Rollins's case, unseasonably cold weather could affect its business, because there is less pest activity in cold weather. But this doesn't concern me so much, because of its global reach and geographical diversity. A major hurricane or other natural disaster could eliminate some of its business, as homes and businesses that are damaged or destroyed will cut off service until they are rebuilt. But once again, Rollins's geographical diversity will mitigate the effects of an adverse weather event on its overall operations. Furthermore, Rollins's business is vulnerable to high fuel costs, because its service personnel drive trucks to service their accounts. But I try not to fret too much over gas prices, because lots of fleet-heavy businesses are harmed by high fuel prices and good managers should be able to manage around this. Another concern would be if consumer sentiment sours on the use of pesticide-based chemicals for health or environmental reasons. But this doesn't concern me so much, because the company already has a green (botanical-based) product offering and it has a top-notch research and development team. My biggest concern is that a new product will prove hazardous to humans or pets.[105]

---

[105] Research for Rollins came from reading company reports that can be found at http://www.rollins.com/annualreports (9/4/2013). I also learned about Rollins while working at Sidoti & Company, an equity research firm that publishes research on Rollins and about 800 other small and medium-size companies.

APPENDIX 5: A VERY, VERY BRIEF REVIEW OF THE BALANCE SHEET AND INCOME STATEMENT

The **balance sheet** is called the balance sheet because it must be balanced at all times, meaning that assets must equal liabilities plus owner's equity (A = L + OE). Companies have two sources of funds: liabilities (debt capital) and equity (owners' capital). So, the liabilities and owner's equity are the "sources" of funds (where the money comes from to purchase the assets) and the asset side of the equation represents the "uses" of funds. Some primary assets include cash, investments (stocks and bonds), inventory (goods sitting on the shelves but not yet sold), and property, plant (factories), and equipment (machinery).

The balance sheet is broken up into current assets and liabilities and long-term assets and liabilities. Current assets include cash, accounts receivable (money owed to the company when customers purchase on credit), and inventories. Current liabilities include accounts payable (money the company owes to it suppliers) and notes payable (debt due within the next year). Net working capital is calculated as current assets minus current liabilities. Net working capital is a measure of the company's short-term liquidity, or its ability to pay short-term bills. Long-term assets are primarily fixed assets (like property, plant, and equipment) and goodwill and intangibles. A company acquires goodwill when it pays more than book value to acquire another company. The amount that the acquirer pays above book value for the target company is recorded as an asset on the acquirer's balance sheet, an asset termed goodwill. Yes, it is a little odd that even if a company pays way too much for another company, that excess is recorded as an asset, but that's just how it's done. There is the risk that if the acquisition does not produce the expected earnings, the goodwill will have to be written down. This is why it is wise to monitor what percentage of a company's total assets is made up of goodwill. Intangibles include things like brand name, patents, trademarks, and client relationships. These assets are termed intangible because they are intangible in nature. Although you can't hold them, they often carry great value. The primary long-term liability is long-term debt.

The balance sheet equation can be rearranged so that total assets minus total liabilities equals shareholders' equity. If a company liquidated all assets to pay off all liabilities, the leftover amount is the company's net worth. The words net worth, book value, and shareholders' equity mean the same thing.

The assets on the balance sheet (things like inventory, machinery, factories, stores, delivery trucks, patents, and trademarks) are used to generate revenues. So now let's take a look at how revenues work their way down the **income statement.**

Sales (revenues) = the top line
<u>minus cost of goods sold</u>
= gross profit
<u>minus operating expenses</u>
= operating income (earnings before interest and taxes)
<u>minus interest expense</u> (note that debt holders are the first to get paid)
= earnings before taxes
<u>minus taxes</u> (note that the government is the second group to get paid)
= net income (note that the shareholders are the last to get paid)

In the above progression you will see that the first group to get paid are the debt holders. The second group to get paid is the government in the form of taxes. The last group to get paid are the shareholders. Whatever is left over after paying the operating expenses of the business (example: wages, marketing, and administrative expenses), paying the interest on the debt, and paying taxes to the government goes solely to the shareholders. This profit available to shareholders is called net income or earnings and is often referred to as the bottom line. Sales are referred to as the top line because it is the top line of the income statement. Earnings are referred to as the bottom line because it is the bottom line of the income statement.

BIBLIOGRAPHY

Graham, Benjamin, and David Dodd. *Security Analysis,* Sixth Edition. New York, NY: McGraw Hill, 2009.

Greenblatt, Joel. *The Little Book That Beats the Market*. Hoboken, NJ: John Wiley & Sons, 2006.

Kaufman, Peter D. *Poor Charlie's Almanack*, Expanded Third Edition. Virginia Beach, VA: The Donning Company Publishers, 2008.

Lynch, Peter. *Beating the Street*. New York, NY: Simon & Schuster, 1993.

Lynch, Peter. *One Up on Wall Street*. New York, NY: Simon & Schuster, 1989.

Marks, Howard. *The Most Important Thing*. New York, NY: Columbia University Press, 2011.

All Warren Buffett letters to shareholders available at www.berkshirehathaway.com.

All Bruce Berkowitz letters available at www.fairholmefunds.com.

OTHER RECOMMENDED READING

Calandro, Joseph. *Applied Value Investing: The Practical Application of Benjamin Graham and Warren Buffett's Valuation Principles to Acquisitions, Catastrophe Pricing, and Business Execution.* New York, NY: McGraw Hill, 2009.

Collins, Jim. *Good to Great.* New York, NY: Harper Collins, 2001.

Cunningham, Lawrence A. *The Essays of Warren Buffett: Lessons for Corporate America.* Second Edition. The Cunningham Group, 2008.

Damodaran, Aswath. *The Little Book of Valuation.* Hoboken, NJ: John Wiley & Sons, 2011.

Fisher, Philip A. *Common Stocks and Uncommon Profits.* Hoboken, NJ: John Wiley & Sons, 2003.

Graham, Benjamin (updated with new commentary by Jason Zweig). *The Intelligent Investor.* New York, NY: Collins Business Essentials, 2003.

Greenblatt, Joel. *You Can Be a Stock Market Genius.* New York, NY: Simon & Schuster, 1997.

Greenwald, Bruce, and Judd Kahn. *Competition Demystified.* New York, NY: Penguin Group, 2005.

Greenwald, Bruce, and Judd Kahn. *Value Investing: From Graham to Buffett and Beyond*. Hoboken, NJ: John Wiley & Sons, 2001.

Hagstrom, Robert G. *Investing: The Last Liberal Art*, Second Edition. New York, NY: Columbia University Press, 2013.

Hagstrom, Robert G. *The Warren Buffett Portfolio*. Hoboken, NJ: John Wiley & Sons, 1999.

Hagstrom, Robert G. *The Warren Buffett Way*. Second Edition. Hoboken, NJ: John Wiley & Sons, 2005.

Jain, Prem C. *Buffett Beyond Value*. Hoboken, NJ: John Wiley & Sons, 2010.

Klarman, Seth. *Margin of Safety*. Out of Print.

Loomis, Carol. *Tap Dancing to Work: Warren Buffett on Practically Everything, 1966-2012*. New York, NY: Penguin Group, 2012.

Lowenstein, Roger. *Buffett: The Making of an American Capitalist*. New York, NY: Broadway Books, 1995.

Lynch, Peter. *Learn to Earn*. New York, NY: Simon & Schuster, 1995.

Marks, Howard. *The Most Important Thing Illuminated*. New York, NY: Columbia University Press, 2013.

Mizrahi, Charles S. *Getting Started in Value Investing*. Hoboken, NJ: John Wiley & Sons, 2008.

Rothchild, John. *The Davis Dynasty*. New York, NY: John Wiley & Sons, 2001.

Schroeder, Alice. *The Snowball: Warren Buffett and the Business of Life*. New York, NY: Bantam Books, 2008.

Schwed, Fred, Jr. *Where Are the Customers' Yachts?* Hoboken, NJ: John Wiley & Sons, 2006.

Thorndike, William N., Jr. *The Outsiders: Eight Unconventional CEOs and Their Radically Rational Blueprint for Success*. Boston, MA: Harvard Business Review Press, 2012.

All Howard Marks memos available at www.oaktreecapital.com.

All Michael Burry letters available at www.scioncapital.com. These letters were available prior to May 11, 2013, but have since been removed from the Internet. Keep an eye out to see if the letters are once again made available to the investing public.

Leucadia National Corporation letters from Ian Cumming and Joseph Steinberg available at http://leucadia.com.

Loews Corporation annual reports available at www.loews.com.

Markel Corporation letters to shareholders available at www.markelcorp.com.

RECOMMENDED SOURCES

The Motley Fool at www.fool.com: The Motley Fool is the home of the three top-performing investment newsletters in the world over the past five years according to the *Hulbert Financial Digest*, and in my opinion, provides the best investment advice and analysis on the Web. I use The Motley Fool to manage my watch list of stocks and check the site daily for news, analysis, and investment ideas. It also provides premium equity research reports. I have a deep respect and admiration for mission-driven companies. There are a few great ones out there. Google is one. Facebook is another. And I think The Motley Fool falls into this category as well. Its mission is to educate, amuse, and enrich. It does all three fabulously.

Hidden Values Alert at www.hiddenvaluesalert.com: This is the monthly value investing newsletter written by my good friend and mentor Charles Mizrahi. Charles is also the author of *Getting Started in Value Investing.* Charles is an excellent stock picker and I highly recommend his book and newsletters. Both his *Hidden Values Alert* and *Inevitable Wealth Portfolio* (http://inevitablewealthportfolio. com/) newsletters are top-rated by the *Hulbert Financial Digest*.

GuruFocus at www.gurufocus.com: GuruFocus tracks what the world's investing gurus are buying and selling, provides 10 years of company data, and offers other commentary and services, including quality monthly newsletters and transcripts of interviews with investing gurus.

Value Line at http://valueline.com: The *Value Line Investment Survey* provides one of the best one-page company snapshots around.

Morningstar at www.morningstar.com: Morningstar provides 10 years of company data at no charge and also provides premium research and screening services for a fee. I consider Morningstar's research to be exceptional, and I especially like its "moat" rating system.

ACKNOWLEDGMENTS

I need to thank many people, some who might not be aware that they played a role in this book (but they did). A word of encouragement or a life lesson well taught can go a very long way.

First of all, I thank my wife, Ana. Ana, without your support and patience, this book would not have been possible. I also thank my parents for doing more than I knew to provide my sisters and me with a top-notch education. Separately I thank my dad for his honesty and my mom for instilling in me the value of living life my way. I am grateful to my sister Ashley for her encouragement and to my sister Tara for keeping my ego in check and never giving me an inch of leeway. If I'm not living up to expectations, Tara makes sure I know it. I love you all dearly.

Next, I thank all the investing superstars who selflessly make themselves available to the public through their writings, interviews, and lectures. I learned to invest from reading your works, and from The Motley Fool and from Robert Hagstrom. Thank you, Tom and David Gardner and all the other Fools for putting out a truly world-class product. Robert, your books do an incredible job of capturing "the Warren Buffett Way," and I consider them to be milestones along my journey as an investor.

I also thank my mentors, Charles Mizrahi and Peter Ricchiuti. Most people would be lucky to have one mentor with your experience and willingness to share that experience. I am nothing short of blessed to have two. You have each been a friend and an advisor, and for that I will be forever grateful. And Charles, you deserve special thanks for advising me on self-publishing and marketing. No one has devoted more time or provided more advice than you.

Professionally, no one has done more for me than Professor Jim Kelly, my boss at the Gabelli Center for Global Investment Analysis. Jim, by allowing me to guest lecture in your classes, you have provided me with an audience to talk about business and investing, and you have given me invaluable career advice as well. I think it's rare to find two people who genuinely enjoy working together and whose skill sets genuinely complement each other. But I feel we have that. The Gabelli Center has a bright future ahead of it with you at the helm, and I am grateful to be a part of it. I also thank Joe Calandro, another world-class educator I met through working at the Gabelli Center. You have also provided invaluable advice on both my career and writing.

I thank Marshall Kaplan and Steve Howard. I hope that one day someone holds me in as high esteem as I hold the two of you. When working on Wall Street I had difficulty finding real friends and people with whom I shared similar values. But I accomplished that with the two of you. You're both successful yet grounded, a very admirable combination. Thank you sincerely for your friendship and support.

I also thank my friend Nick Belfanti for doing one final proofread of my manuscript before I sent it off to be published. I appreciate the time and attention you gave to the book, given your busy schedule. You identified parts of the book that needed further explanation and by doing so I know you have enhanced the reader experience. You're a very capable analyst, and your edits and suggestions were very much appreciated.

I thank all my friends from home, college, and business school. I've learned so much from each of you, and other than my family, no one has played a bigger role in shaping who I am. So you deserve some of the greatest thanks of all.

Finally, I thank the readers. I believe that learning is a two-way street. Please email me with any thoughts, questions, or suggestions you may have to jlrpotlucklearning@gmail.com.

ABOUT THE AUTHOR

John L. Rotonti, Jr., is a private investor and a Fellow at the Gabelli Center for Global Investment Analysis, where he works closely with the director in developing new programs and events for the Center. He graduated Phi Beta Kappa and magna cum laude from the University of Richmond and received an MBA from the Tulane Freeman School of Business, where he graduated as a member of the Beta Gamma Sigma International Business Honors Society. While at Tulane he interned at Stifel Nicolaus and was a research assistant for the Burkenroad Equity Research Program. After graduating from Tulane, he worked in the family business and later in institutional equity sales at Sidoti & Company, a premier small-cap equity research firm. He has given guest lectures at both the Gabelli School of Business and Tulane University on topics ranging from value investing to analyzing banks and insurance companies. He is currently working on a second book, which he hopes to publish in early 2015.

Made in the USA
San Bernardino, CA
21 September 2014